CW00521691

CONTE**NTS**

Preface v

Introduction ix

Wendy Stunt 1

Alan Hennessy 5

Don Harris 10

Bibi Baskin 15

Jill Lush 18

Alison Arngrim 21

Gerry Creighton 25

Loretta Dignam and Henny Flynn 31

Sinead Tynan Byrne 44

Rob Cullen 52

Liz Sheehan 58

Marguerite Penrose 63

Rachel Thornburgh 71

Ciairín De Buis 77

Seán Kelly 81

Keith Kelly 85

Billy Kilkenny 94

Sharon Tregenza 99

Rachel Gotto 103

Howard Hughes 112

Russ Hedge 121

Pamela Finn 125

Irial O'Farrell 129

Jeremy Murphy. 137

Patrick Osborne 141

Wendy Slattery 146

Michelle Maher 150

Catherine Thompson 155

Lorraine Keane 158

Mona Lydon-Rochelle 162

Jennifer Carroll MacNeill 166

Stephan Murtagh 170

Lucy Wolfe 175

Simon Acton 179

Aoife Ryan 184

Muriel Bolger 190

Aoife Mollin. 193

PREFACE

*A*h yes, the casual acquaintance ...

Those peripheral friends we meet at the bus stop, the gym, the coffee shop; friendships founded on convenience, always good for a natter about this and that and nothing at all. Friendships that might span years, and yet never get beyond first names or a throw-away comment regarding a change in the weather. Then one day, when you least expect it, you find yourself facing one of life's insurmountable challenges – and there's your casual acquaintance, standing beside you, with a hand of support stretched out in your direction. That's when you realise that there's nothing casual about casual acquaintances, and life is far less a game of chance than we sometimes like to think it is.

The convenience of acquaintances was something we all took for granted in those halcyon days before Covid cast a cold cape of self-imposed isolation across the land. But such is the tenacity of human spirit that despite lockdowns and social distancing we continued to reach out to virtual strangers. Yvonne Reddin and I were not virtual strangers, we were in fact virtual friends – connected across the social media platform LinkedIn.

A post on Yvonne's timeline grabbed my attention. I shared some opinions on the nature of e-books and indie publishing – and so the conversation began. And just like that, our virtual acquaintance took root and over time has blossomed into a real-life friendship.

Casual acquaintances in the virtual world come relatively fully formed with profile photo and biography attached. So, it soon became apparent to me that Yvonne was a busy woman, an energetic woman, one of life's natural creatives and a woman of many interests. And though she possessed more than a passing passion for fashion and clothes design, life-choices guided her along another path.

Yvonne's fascination for sourcing a good story and peeling back the concealing layers of the human condition inspired her to take a degree in journalism, and the completion of a captivating thesis exploring The Freedom of Information Act and how it benefited journalism.

Notwithstanding Yvonne's natural fascination in finding a good story, she also has a deep 'yearning for learning' – and this motivated her to complete a Postgraduate degree on teaching further education. Her dual expertise in journalism and teaching further education dovetailed together seamlessly in the creation of this published work – Talk Learn Connect [TLC].

Interestingly, Talk Learn Connect [TLC] began life as Teach Learn Care [TLC] a practical hands-on, bespoke teaching program, designed to create a safe and caring environment that would reintroduce adults to the benefits of further education. But the unprecedented, unexpected shock waves of the Global Pandemic scuppered any plans she had to proceed with that particular project.

March 2020, the world as we knew it had stopped spinning, post-apocalyptic images of deserted cities in lockdown flashed up on our TV screens. It was a time of reassessment, soul searching and self-analysis. Yvonne found her journalistic experience began to take precedence, and though her initial project had been envisioned as a practical educational tool, over time Talk Learn Connect became a creative expression of her life-long deep interest in the human story, the human spirit and ultimately the human condition. Somewhere between the transition from practical project to published page, Talk Learn Connect [TLC] materialised as an emotional engagement.

Like all brilliant ideas, Yvonne's publication is based on a very simple concept. Through her LinkedIn connections she identified over thirty individuals from various backgrounds and walks of life – and having developed a profile piece she pitched each individual five questions.

It soon became apparent that this project was far more than a response to the isolation of lockdown, Yvonne was digging deep into the human psyche, each individual offering a unique insight into the person behind their brand.

The five questions posed by Yvonne presented an equal unbiased template, but each interviewee was at liberty to expand their response into sharing personal real-life human-interest stories. During the various conversations a most engaging and intriguing array of subject matter was explored and discussed – including, adoption, post-traumatic stress disorder, multiple sclerosis, mental health, menopause – the full gamut of life's experience.

Talk Learn Connect [TLC] is not an educational-tool - it is a creative sharing of experience, a memoir of different voices, a learning experience of people from various walks of life. This publication presents a wealth of experience – a journey paved with resilience, tenacity and survival. The stories told and explored between the covers of this book are of value and need to be shared with as wide an audience as possible. At its core, this story is a journey to the human soul, It is a journey I would highly recommend you take.

Cónal Creedon
Adjunct Professor Creative Writing UCC.
Cónal is a novelist, playwright and documentary film maker.

INTRODUCTION

Freelance Writer, Content and Story Creator, Interviewer, Mammy of three amazing children (Finn, Connie, Sonny)

$\mathcal{W}$hat is it about a person's story that catches your attention? Is it their character, achievements, challenges they speak publicly about, life experiences, or their ability to capture an audience telling their story vocally? For me, it's all of this and more.

We can buy books, hear people on the radio, watch them on our screens but for me it is about the stories you don't hear. Stories from our neighbours, our mentors, our friends and our peers. We know our elevator pitches, but I want to know, what is it that drives - You - the person behind the brand.

This collection of interviews is the result of a project I developed during the many lockdowns and isolation periods of the global pandemic. I began to connect with people across social media platforms and wanted to learn more about business, book marketing, author interviews, coaching, copy writing, mentors, tutors, women in politics – the list goes on.

There is no doubt, there is something here for everyone and I hope you might learn something new or find a new contact with similar interests and continue this connection cycle.

Talk Learn Connect or TLC, is a softer style, profile piece using a five-question format, designed and researched for the interviewee.

I learned and connected with my guests, and I am now sharing these interviews with you, so you can learn and connect also.

Enjoy this book and share with people far and wide. We have learned throughout this global pandemic – connection and community are so valuable in our lives.

WENDY STUNT

Visionary Consultant & Director Go DigiCard

Contact:

Website: www.godigicard.com
LinkedIn: Wendy Stunt

*C*an you explain what a new customer can expect from a Visionary Consultant and how you utilize your knowledge to assist businesses/clients?

For me, it's all about seeing something that is transparent to me that a client doesn't see. My clients are amazed when my vision and analysis are put in front of them, and they then recognise what part of their business needs to be adjusted.

It can sometimes be as simple as changing social media platforms, outsourcing to a graphic designer and perhaps an introduction to a contact I have that may be beneficial to both clients.

People who know me, know I love connecting people and more importantly I love to hear what people are doing and where they need help. The networking side to the business is as important as doing your accounts. If you don't network, how will people know what you do?

I have built up a vast contact network that has taken me years. I went to many networking events and got to know people from all professions and that contact base is part of my business now.

But you know I can't give away all my secrets. You will have to hire me to see how I can enhance your business.

"I'm a firm believer in 'Being Stronger Together'"

You won Entrepreneur of the Year 2019, what are the different mindsets of a successful self-employed person and that of an entrepreneur?

Entrepreneurs are always thinking of new ways of innovation whereas a self-employed business owner generally has one business and concentrates on that one. It's really a very different mindset when you look at it in this way. I have had several businesses, and all were a learning experience.

I find within 2-3 years, I get itchy feet and I move on to another idea, to see how I can make it successful. I would definitely say I am a serial entrepreneur.

I feel a need to help everybody and always put myself last. I work as a consultant with companies and take them on a journey and once that we have fulfilled our objective, I move on to my next client.

Business creativity is something that comes naturally to me, and I have plenty of experience since my twenties to know if a business is going to work or not. I don't like to stay with a venture when there is no movement or change happening. It has to be about moving to another level, if it's not moving, I move on. It's that simple.

How has your business managed throughout the pandemic, have you had to pivot your business with new strategies?

My business hasn't pivoted but my client's businesses have. I have found that I have stepped more into the role of a mentor and supporting my clients in their business. I believe in a "Being Stronger Together" attitude. When the pandemic began, I could see businesses going under, but I could also see the potential for collaboration opportunities to save businesses also.

Why should businesses go under when perhaps we could come together and share what we need and see how we could also support each other. Little did we know nearly two years later, we would still be in this position.

Not everyone has been able to pivot successfully but bringing people together on zoom networking groups, is what saved and helped many people, it still is.

I don't think the zoom culture is going anywhere, it's here to stay.

Can you think of any positives that may arise from this unforeseen, economic catastrophe, from a business perspective?

Most business owners are working 24/7 and always have been. Really, we were going around in circles, trying to keep our heads above water. The hybrid model that we are hearing everywhere will benefit us all. I mean, did people enjoy the crazy hours they were working? So many people were working to live instead of actually living.

Now we have had time to look at all these situations and prioritise them. Some people have really stopped, embraced the hybrid model and slowed down.

The pandemic certainly made us all rethink our professional and personal lives and what matters most. There must be a positive in all this somewhere.

Can you share any words of wisdom that you received that helped you in your successful career?

I love the quote from Mother Theresa - "I alone cannot change the world, but I can cast a stone across the water to create many ripples."

I hope I have been helpful and supportive to many, and I also like it reciprocated. People I have around me now are loyal and have my best interests to heart and to me that matters the most. You need that support group around you to keep you grounded.

My good friend Don Harris has advised me so well in his mentoring and I can say this if you haven't already - go and get a mentor or coach, it is worth every penny. Don broke everything down for me and definitely helped me see clearly.

And not to forget Alan Hennessy - The Digital Mentor, who shared his invaluable knowledge and time with me. Last but not least your good self, my great friend and partner in crime, have been a constant support and the best craic for the last two years while building our businesses. The three of us have laughed over so many long zoom calls throughout the pandemic and I think we got each other through the last 18 months

ALAN HENNESSY

The Digital Mentor - Kompass Media

Contact:

Website: www.kompassmedia.ie
LinkedIn: alanhennessy
Twitter: Kompassmedia

*C*an you give the Talk Learn Connect (TLC) audience a summary of your professional path?

I'm a digital mentor and marketing consultant, podcaster and LinkedIn expert. I help solo entrepreneurs and business owners to navigate the digital landscape and break through the noise of social media to help them create visibility and build awareness for their brand. I've been in this profession for fifteen years and I also have two very successful podcasts.

My two podcasts are quite different - the Social Media Talks Podcast is where I talk to some of the world's leading experts in digital marketing, social media and business. The other podcast - the Curious Fire, I co-host with my good friend Trevor Lorkings.

This is more of a passion of mine and delves into subjects that are a bit off-center, but they are topics that people don't ask. Topics like procrastination, digital dopamine, our thoughts and the wisdom of age and we have conversations about them.

So, you can see the two podcasts have very different content and I like that variety of conversation.

You have interviewed a range of guests for your podcasts, what or who inspires you?

Many years ago, I heard a quote that I think is brilliant and it sums up what I do and what I believe in - 'Your only limitation is you.' I think it's so true because we limit ourselves and we seem to say, we can't do something that we can actually do.

There would be several people including Simon Sinek or Mark Schaefer that I aspire to. Simon Sinek has a way of speaking the truth and his explanation of understanding life and your own ideas of life. Mark Schaefer looks at a subject and develops it in such a way that the reader can understand it and we all learn from it.

I was fascinated by his book - The Marketing Rebellion: The Most Human Company Wins. It changed my perception and vision for marketing because he came at it from a different angle. It was so insightful and a pleasure to read.

"When I began my podcast, I remember one of the best pieces of advice I got was when I interviewed Ted Rubin. I was quite nervous interviewing him because he was such a celebrity, an innovator and a marketer of global standings"

When I got on the podcast, he actually came off from another interview about Amazon on CNN News, he came on, and said, "Sorry for being late, I was just finishing an interview on CNN news."

I said to him that really has made me a little bit more nervous and his exact words to me and it's the advice that I've carried through with everything I do is that "It's just the two of us having a chat, person to person, friend to friend."

I will always remember that because we are all doing the same things just in different ways. It really resonated with me, and I've carried that through in everything I do in regard to training, business and people I have met in my life.

Your work is primarily Digital Mentorship, what are your views on the future of social media?

I think social media gets bad publicity and it has for a while because it's portrayed a lot as being very destructive - and it can be. But it can also be used in such a positive, productive way. It brings so many people together. It helps us to build solid relationships, connect with people that we would never have been able to connect with. We can now understand how people are thinking.

We understand how people are feeling from what they are uploading, and it gives us the ability to nurture relationships. I think, social media going forward, will see a huge shift and if you are to succeed on social you need to connect with your audience. You will need to listen to what they are saying and also see how you can reach out and help solve the problems that they have. The social media landscape has changed from just predominantly based promotion to connecting with your followers on a human level and engaging with them.

"There will be more structure in personal connections over the next number of years where it's not going to be about the brand, it's going to be about the people that are behind these brands"

There will be more inclusivity with the people involved in social media. It will also give companies a huge opportunity to show the human side of what they do. It's very similar to what you do here with your Talk Learn Connect series, we find out more about the person behind the brand. People we never thought approachable are now on their social media platforms interacting with their audience.

So, social media will keep growing and is not going anywhere, it's part of our lives and is powerful once we utilise it in the right way.

Can you give any advice to people considering the path of digital marketing or podcasting?

The biggest piece of advice I can offer, is to understand where it is that you want to concentrate your efforts on. This means finding your niche and audience, understanding it, absorb your craft and keep developing it every day.

Going forward, don't just say, "I know it all," because none of us do. It is so important that we keep learning new things.

And understand the industry that we are in, it's forever changing, so there's continuous updates, new concepts and new behaviours to keep up with. When I started first, it was all images, this has advanced quickly to video content. It has pivoted and it's changing on a daily basis.

So, I would say pick your niche and work with it and become the expert in that field. Never stop learning, stay ahead in your profession.

DON HARRIS

The Active Listening & Speaking Coach/Mentor

Contact:

Website: Talkback
LinkedIn: Don Harris
Podcast: Listening is the Business

*C*ould you give a summary of your varied, professional career to date?

I began my career in a major retail store in Dublin called Switzers where I first learned how to deal with customers, which is different from dealing with 'people.' Maybe this is where I first understood about being a good listener. I certainly came across a range of situations I had never experienced before, including some serious shoplifting!

I also worked with the RNLI in Ireland as Deputy National Organiser and often thought I should have stayed a few more years. It was one of my favourite jobs and I stayed there for over 3 years.

I have been a broadcaster for over 30 years in different radio presenting roles on various independent radio stations.

I was the first CEO of Independent Radio Sales (IRS) established in 1992 - I was the founder and Chairperson of The National Radio Advertising Awards which became the PPI's – currently the major Awards for excellence in broadcasting in radio, the IMRO's. I am especially proud of this achievement which began in 1993.

Currently, I am now a Podcaster although in the early stages and I am fully focused on my life calling to be an Executive Coach (since 2009) and Tour Guide. Both pursuits require more than a little Active Listening. I personally get a lot out of helping people find their own direction, in more ways than one.

"Active listening is a valuable technique that requires the listener to thoroughly absorb, understand, respond, and retain what's being said." (ccl.org)

Can you explain, in your words, what is involved in your work as a 'Listening Coach'?

I believe a person must turn up fully attuned to the person in front of them, to be able to listen to them properly. Then you can offer them support or just the opportunity to be listened to. My work involves spending time with management and employees to assist an organisation to be more engaged with their employees, leading to better productivity.

The company management must first realise there is an issue before embarking on this project. Trust may have broken down or simply been almost non-existent. My role can sometimes be to restore that trust which takes time. Most importantly action by the organisation's management to fix the issues raised is the positive end result. Very often I am asked to implement a program to ensure the changes required are taking place and check-in thereafter that no slippage happens.

"Measurement is crucial before, during and after."

Through TalkBack and CoachTalk, I work focusing on how people interact, listen, talk and communicate. My passion is for leading people towards discovering their strengths and identifying areas where the scope for development may be unearthed. I advocate more Empathy at Work and the importance of Emotional Intelligence at work.

My online workshop 'Listening is The Business' opens minds and souls and highlights the importance of giving others the opportunity to be listened to at work, as well as socially.

If we delve into the science of listening, it is more complex than you think. We often hear the expression, "he/she is a great listener" but how do you differentiate a good listener from an average one? When it comes to talking more and opening dialogue lines— it all starts with a conversation. And to have a meaningful conversation, we need to listen to each other.

If we look closer at the four types of listening:

Deep Listening - occurs when you are dedicated to understanding the narrator's viewpoint.

Full Listening - is when you are paying close consideration to what the speaker is communicating.

Critical Listening - is when you evaluate and give your opinion on the narrator's thoughts or views.

Therapeutic Listening - is the use of music or sensory techniques applied to a particular need.

In my coaching, I listen to my clients, understand their dialogue and I give my feedback accordingly to the conversation. Sometimes an outside 'listener' can be valuable to a company or a new business owner, to help and support them on their venture into business. Yes, it is important to have conversations, but listening is also necessary for dialogue development.

The combination of coaching and Empathetic Listening skills is a powerful formula for delivering extraordinary results in greater pro-ductivity and one I am proud to be able to deliver.

My work allows me the opportunity and privilege to meet some out-standing people who feel that nobody at work is listening to them or interested in their views. Sadly, in some cases that's true – company morale often reaches rock bottom as a result.

In your opinion, what are the main elements that any business owner should always remember?

If the company does not demonstrate a genuine caring attitude to its people, why on earth would the people have any interest in the future of the company.

It's far more likely they will look for alternative employment.

From listening to your clients, what has been the main aspect in the significant shift in the way we will live and work in the future?

There is a major move towards the hybrid option for employees around home working and time spent in the office HQ. Companies are going to have to put in place workable solutions to keep their employees involved in a manner that works for all.

Burnout is a major topic now aligned with mental health issues. Every company must take a hard look at how it sees itself communicating with its workforce and this is where I can help.

Can you share any words of wisdom that you received that helped you in your successful career?

I once asked to have a word with my boss in a publishing company. I seemed to be having a bad day, nothing was going right.

My boss said to me - 'Don, at lunchtime, go up to the children's hospital (not far away) and walk around the children's wards and come back to me and then tell me you're still having a bad day.'

I've never forgotten those words and have used the example on more than one occasion with some of my coaching clients.

It's a question of perspective.

BIBI BASKIN

Radio Presenter, Hotelier and
former Television Presenter

Contact:

Website: www.bibibaskin.ie
Twitter: @BibiBaskin
Podcast: Bibi's Wellness Wisdom

*W*hile presenting your TV/Radio shows, can you share some stories from guests that you will remember for both positive and negative reasons?

My show was crafted and designed to have an overall positive contour. It was non-aggressive in tone. There were so many special moments but in particular, I remember the great tenor, Jose Carreras.

When I asked him what the last thing was, he thought about as he was walking from backstage out front in La Scala, he replied "My

mother." It was very touching and gave me the perfect moment at which to end the interview.

India has a special place in your heart, and you spent a lot of time there, can you tell us why you were drawn there and your association with India now?

I ostensibly went to India on a three-week holiday. But I stayed for a little longer – fifteen years!

I went to further my knowledge of the Indian system of Wellness, Ayurveda, which I had been studying unofficially in Ireland and in the UK for about ten years previously.

I afterward became a hotelier there. Today I am still very much in touch with India because like everyone else who loves India, it has an inescapable pull on you forever.

Before Covid, I used to go there once a year and always to my old stomping ground, Kerala.

Your career has spanned a range of diverse professions, which one has brought you the most fulfillment, and why?

They were all fulfilling because when the enjoyment faded, I moved on to something new.

We are slowly returning to a new 'normal', how did you find the pandemic affected you in relation to your wellness and indeed your everyday life?

I was very lucky with the pandemic. Firstly, I haven't got ill.

And after that, the new lifestyle occasioned by lockdown and then by restricted movements fell inline very easily with where I prefer to be.

That is, at home! I have spent the time studying, learning, and writing. And I just may continue!

Can you share any words of wisdom that helped you in your successful career?

Oddly enough, and perhaps it's an age thing, but I have never had a mentor.

I have never had advice from anyone along the way. I'm very accustomed to making decisions alone.

But I could give a little advice – something which I use all the time in my Motivational talks – "Never let fear of failure hold you back."

JILL LUSH

Digital Marketer

Contact:

Website: www.lushmarketing.ie

*C*an you share a summary of your career to where you are currently?

I studied Business and Marketing in DCU and loved the marketing subjects. I knew that I eventually wanted to work in the marketing area. I also completed the Graduate programme in AIB and thought I'd stay there for six months but left seventeen years later!

I worked for my final five years in Group Marketing and found my love of working with businesses as I worked in the Business propositions area.

I was involved in the development of the business website for AIB and the AIB Startup Academy in conjunction with the Irish Times.

When I left AIB in 2017, I started studying my Postgrad in Digital Marketing with the Digital Marketing Institute. That same year, I had my little girl. I was juggling study, starting a new business and being a mum to a newborn.

I am currently working with small and medium businesses, mentoring and training this sector in marketing. I also provide marketing strategy and marketing outsourcing services.

What do you consider when developing marketing strategies and training for SME's?

- Definitely their target customer
- Their brand values
- Their strengths and weaknesses
- A situation analysis
- Competitor analysis

In your experience, what do businesses not take notice of more, in terms of marketing, that is vital for their business?

For me when I am the outsider looking in, it is often that they are not taking enough notice of their ideal customer.

Is there a person or multiple individuals, that you admire and think that they are way ahead of the global market and have a unique vision?

In terms of businesses, I admire companies like Amazon for their customer centricity and Lego for their timelessness.

Coca Cola and the larger brands interest me but I also love watching Irish brands like Keoghs growing from strength to strength.

Can you share any words of wisdom?

To always be true to myself. There is no point in being something or someone that you're not. Always be authentic.

ALISON ARNGRIM

Actress, Author, Stand-up Comedian

Contact:

Website: www.alisonarngrim.net
Twitter: @Arngrim
Instagram: Alison Arngrim

*Y*ou were born to be on the stage, it's in your family genes, but if you had not gone down the path of acting, what do you think you would have chosen as a profession?

Good question! I'm not sure, I definitely enjoy talking to people and I'm fascinated by how the human mind works, so acting might still have been a possibility.

Although, in high school, I became very interested in psychology and seriously considered pursuing a degree and becoming a therapist or psychiatrist.

From listening to your conversation on the Women's Inspire Network virtual conference in October 2020, you are the queen of reinvention, how many times do you think you have reinvented yourself?

Hahaha! Oh, seven or eight times at least! Honestly, it started in childhood.

I had totally reinvented myself when I was on Little House as a twelve-year-old girl in order to not let my shyness stand in the way of working with others on the set. As an actor or any kind of performer, you need to stay 'current 'and 'relevant'.

That can be a lot of work, but I have managed to adapt to the circumstances over and over again.

Your comedy act is a huge hit in France, would you bring your show to Ireland Post Covid and have you any deep connections here?

Oh yes! That would be great!

And I HAVE TO get over there at some point, to see the home of my ancestors! Like many Americans, I'm of Irish descent, my father's birth name was Wilfred James Bannin.

I'm on Ancestry and all that!

Did you find it liberating writing your book "Confessions of a Prairie Bitch: How I Survived Nellie Oleson and Learned to Love Being Hated"?

Yes. Thankfully it wasn't the first time I had EVER talked about these things.

I had many, many years of therapy, which I think is a good thing. I know a lot of people feel that writing an autobiography IS therapy, but I think it can be dangerous, emotionally and psychologically to just jump in and "tell all" without having worked through the heavier issues with a professional of some kind.

And of course, I'd been telling bits and pieces of my life story on stage in my one woman show for a while.

But to see all those stories come together and see the reaction of readers was VERY rewarding.

I grew up as did many, watching Little House on the Prairie. I have to ask; did you love playing the boldest child in the village and tell us more about your Walnut Grove family? Were you sad to see it end?

YES! I admit, I LOVED playing Nellie Oleson! It was so much fun to say and do all those terrible things that I would never do in real life! LOL

And indeed, the set of Little House was a very supportive environment. Wonderful people. And unlike most shows in Hollywood, the cast of Little House all still speak to each other! LOL

When it ended, I had mixed feelings. In some ways I was glad to be grownup and 'done' with it - I had been there seven years! - but yes, I knew I would miss being there with my friends every day.

I think that's why I'm so glad we still speak and interact on Twitter and Facebook.

Alison, can you share any words of wisdom that you received that helped you in your successful career?

Oh, so many! Between my crazy manager father and all the people I've met in Hollywood, I've definitely collected a lot of advice.

Appreciating what's happening right now and trying to limit how stressed out you get about the future - as my father put it - "You could be hit by a bus tomorrow!"

GERRY CREIGHTON

Global Elephant Care Consultant

Contact:

Instagram: gerry.creighton
Facebook: Global Elephant Care

*C*ould you share where your love of animals, in particular the elephants, began?

I was lucky to be a second-generation zookeeper, my father worked at the zoo for 52 years. As a young boy, I went up to the zoo every weekend from the age of 5/6, it was like my own private playground.

It was one of the best parts of growing up with the other keeper's kids and the freedom of walking around the zoo among these magnificent animals.

I always envisaged working with animals, it held a particular magnetism, the sights, and the smells that you came into contact with from a young age.

To see these powerful cats and majestic elephants, I couldn't wait to get out of school to begin my zoo career.

It was all I wanted to do and after 36 years working in Dublin Zoo, there has never been a single day I didn't look forward to going to work.

"Elephants are the largest existing land animals" – How important is it to you to educate and share your knowledge on a global level?

It's hugely important because elephants are a unique part of the ecosystem, if elephants thrive, the whole environment thrives. They pass seeds in their dung that rejuvenate forests that make plants grow, their big footprints they leave in the muddy sand where a pool can form from the depression of the foot; frogs can leave their spawn there and it can be developed.

They are incredibly important to the landscape and the environment that they live in. They have been so badly treated by humans because of their charisma and strength. We have always wanted to

be so close to them and prepared to keep them, under any circumstances.

I want to make people understand the empathy, the emotive intelligence, the integrity of the herd, the kindness that they have towards one another and how they manage the family unit, to create a progressive future for the whole herd.

We need to look at the whole area of injustice we have done to them by keeping them in conditions and the cultural countries where they come from like in India where they still use temples, and they are chained up for long periods of time.

What do you feel is the next step to shifting the narrative on elephant care from a controlled belief to a more habitual one?

The method of free contact control for an elephant is devastating because you have something that looks like an elephant, its grey, has a trunk but emotionally and physically, it becomes bankrupt.

We become the dominant person in its life, we do its thinking. It becomes a relationship based on fear and there should be no consequence for any animal when a human or keeper comes into their world and its life is threatened. They shouldn't feel under pressure that if it doesn't conform and do what's right, that there will be a consequence for the animal.

The modern zookeeper or elephant keeper is like an architect of the habitat creating choice and opportunities for the elephant to express throughout the day, creating typography landscapes, looking at the biology of the elephant – how they exist, how they live, how they function in harmony with their anatomy.

We need to make sure they have the ability of expression to live an authentic life, free from fear. That's why it's so important to educate people about the sensitivity and intelligence of these animals.

Can you share how and why the bond between mother and daughter elephants, is unique and unbreakable - it sounds genuinely extraordinary.

It is extraordinary - the core of elephant society is the mother and daughter, which is the whole function of the family. That is the unbreakable bond – their unique relationship. The mother brings the daughter into a birthing process where the mother is giving her daughter an education into the natural process.

This allows the daughter to mature into a breeding female that has respect and integrity in the herd. It's about how they care for one another, the whole herd comes around a young elephant, they put the calves in the middle to protect them - it's all about the future of the herd. The bull elephants are extraordinarily different, from the moment they are born, they are designed to leave the herd.

They have a different makeup. You would see a bull drifting a few 100 meters from its mother after a couple of days, you would never see that with the female. It's almost like the umbilicus has been moved to outside the body. It's an extraordinary relationship and a joy to watch and see that lifelong bond.

It goes the opposite way too, when the older matriarch gets older, the younger females will help her, supporting and guiding her, shorten their journeys for her and make sure she has food.

They are truly an incredible species in terms of their integrity and their loyalty to each other.

Can you share any words of wisdom that you received that helped you in your successful career?

I have had many people who have had a positive influence on my life in terms of the zoo.

My father Gerry Creighton Senior was way before his time and very progressive in his thinking. Even though he came from an era where animals were in the old lion houses in the zoo and kept in confined spaces, he was always thinking forward in his thought process of introducing substrates to the floors of the primates.

Substrates were bark chippings and food items could be hidden and found. Also, Alan Roocroft has been a great mentor for elephants to me for the last 25 years.

He has worked with elephants for five decades and has evolved from the old free contact dominating person dominating the animals to understanding that these animals can thrive in our care. What we have learned in zoos is the more you step away from them, the more appropriate elephant behaviour you will receive.

But also, words of wisdom are to respect the animals for what they are - they are wild animals. Even though they are formidable, strong, sensitive, have empathy and emotional intelligence; they respect and tend to do anything for real meaning – the integrity of the herd and to protect their young, their environment, and their territory.

"Respect is the keyword in all areas of care
and understanding of elephants and
all animals in general."

LORETTA DIGNAM AND HENNY FLYNN

CEO of The Menopause Hub | ACC Accredited
Coach and Speaker

Contact Loretta Dignam:

Website:www.themenopausehub.ie

Contact Henny Flynn:

Website: www.hennyflynn.co.uk

*C*an you share your story from when you began having some symptoms to how you managed to control and to live with menopause?

Henny:

I think it was 2010 (I was about 40) when I first went to the doctor to say I thought I might be peri menopausal. I didn't really know what the word meant but I knew it was something to do with the

menopause, and what leads up to it. I was still menstruating - albeit randomly - but I felt odd. I knew I wasn't myself and just had a sense that something else was going on.

Like many women, although the doctor was lovely, I was told I was far too young. I seem to recall she did some bloods to check if anything else was going on but there wasn't, and so that was the end of it.

I just carried on.

Things got progressively worse. But because I'd been told it 'Definitely wasn't menopause' I looked to other causes for my symptoms and for ways to suppress or alleviate them.

By 2015, I was also dealing with deep grief, severe stress at work and a body that I thought was no longer my own. Constant aching, unexplained weight gain, hot flushes, foggy head, loss of confidence... All beautifully suppressed by working even harder, as a way of avoiding dealing with things that felt too painful.

I still had no support and none of my girlfriends seemed to be going through it at the same time - or at least we didn't realise it.

Then in 2016, I had three bouts of pneumonia. The last one nearly finished me off for good and I finally realised that something had to change - That something was me. Then followed an intense time of personal change. Nothing is the same now as it was then. I created a bedrock of self-care which led to an even deeper sense of self-love which I had been missing all my life.

It was this decision to care for myself, on the deepest level, that enabled me to move forward.

By changing my nutrition, my self-talk, my mind-set, by opening up to new people and new experiences, by accessing new knowledge - by allowing myself to be truly self-aware and self-compassionate - I changed my experience of menopause, completely.

Two of the key practices I adopted were meditation and journaling, both things I still do pretty much every day. The journaling led to writing a series of love letters to myself, helping me see and hear my own inner wisdom.

And (this is still very new) through a series of happy accidents, they've now become a book called My Darling Girl.

And the same question for Loretta Dignam Founder and CEO of The Menopause Hub

Loretta:

Unfortunately, my knowledge of menopause was limited to hot flushes or flashes (as they say in the US) and the end of periods. I knew nothing about perimenopause and had never even heard the word, such was my lack of awareness and education about the topic. And as I have learned, I am not alone. From market research I have conducted, eighty per cent of women in Ireland are unprepared for menopause. (Source: online research, Sept & Oct 2020, 1132, respondents)

So, the first I knew I was menopausal was a month before I turned fifty, when my periods stopped and then the hot flushes began (the average age of menopause is fifty-one). It was a shock and surprise to me, as I had expected menopause to hit me when I was older... maybe late fifties. Isn't that an older woman's thing? Of course, like many women, I was terrified of HRT. I thought it would give me breast cancer and was for women who couldn't 'power through' menopause - so to be avoided completely.

More ignorance and lack of education! So instead, I tried everything 'natural'- cut down on tea and coffee, cut down on alcohol, increased my exercise and tried natural remedies, such as, sage, black cohosh, evening primrose oil and vitamins. I even bought a magnet in Boots pharmacy for thirty-five euro, which is supposed to help with menopausal symptoms.

I had to put it in my underwear. But the only thing that happened to me was that the wire baskets in the supermarket and the chains on the shopping trollies stuck to my underwear and caused me major embarrassment! My menopausal symptoms continued, unabated.

Eventually, after three years of hot flushes, where I could not get my clothes off quick enough, make-up sliding off my face and damp hair - I 'gave in' and went to see my GP. I was exhausted. The symptoms were relentless. I felt like a slow puncture, the energy slowly seeping out of me. When would this end??? Apparently, the average length of time of menopause is 7.4 years between peri and post-menopause.

But, once again, I was unaware of that. My GP visit was short and sweet. No periods and hot flushes – I was post-menopausal (post-menopausal is when a woman is one year without her periods, and she remains post-menopausal for the rest of her life. Anything before that is peri-menopausal).

So, my female GP reassured me that the risks of breast cancer from HRT was much lower than the 2002 Women's Health Initiative

Study had led us to believe. She prescribed a combined hormone patch for me, with oestrogen and progesterone in it. I left knowing nothing more about menopause than the first two facts I knew when I went in.

Some weeks later, I took off the patch and went elsewhere for advice. This was a completely different consultation, much longer and much more expensive, where I learned about the impact of declining oestrogen on my body. I then learned that my oestrogen had been declining throughout my forties when I was peri menopausal.

The UTIs I had continuously were not a coincidence, the headaches (where I had to go for an MRI scan to rule out sinister causes) the asthma development, the fatigue, the dizziness, the dry eye (where I ended up three times in the Eye and Ear Emergency Department) the pains in my ankles, the palpitations, the ten pound weight gain, the night sweats, the dry skin, the leaks when I coughed, laughed or sneezed, the getting up to go to the loo during the night, the loss of confidence, the brain fog, the memory loss, the loss of va va voom the disappearing eyebrows, the chin hair… I had better stop there.

Oh, and of course the hot flushes, up to thirty a day every day and at night. The one thing that I did not suffer, which I know a lot of women experience, is anxiety. Lucky me.

I was prescribed separate hormones, oestrogen, progesterone and testosterone. And within a few weeks, the symptoms improved. I had my dosage of hormones adjusted after three months and I have never looked back. I got my 'old self' back. My life was changed for the better and so I decided to set up The Menopause Hub to help change other women's lives.

For many women, there is a lack of awareness around menopause but there is a great deal of information out there, where would you recommend women to begin researching?

Henny:

There are two aspects to this I believe. One is the external research and reaching out to communities that resonate with the experience you want to create for yourself.

The other is reaching in, and asking yourself, what do you most need... what's the kindest thing you can do for yourself right now... what does your inner wisdom have to say? The point about choosing our community is SO critical. When we're surrounded by positive voices and support, it builds our resilience in a compassionate way.

And that enables us to make clearer choices about the experience we want to have. In terms of where to look for practical information - that stretches across a really wide range of topics and themes - I would say the MPowder community on Instagram is a beautiful place to start. I'm their resident life coach, and I work with them for a reason. Diane Danzebrink's work is also great for very practical discussions and tools.

I would recommend having a look at Christiane Northrup's book, Women's Bodies, Women's Wisdom - a medical doctor with a refreshingly open mind.

Loretta:

50% of the population will go through menopause at some stage. Yet menopause is still a taboo topic. Women in Ireland rated the level of taboo at seven out of ten, in our most recent survey.

Yet, there are 571,000 women in Ireland in the menopausal age group (45-65) according to the 2016 Census. And even more if we include those women who are in premature menopause, early menopause and surgical menopause.

80% are unprepared for menopause - 80% will have symptoms - 45% will have moderate to severe symptoms - 25% will have severe symptoms - 25% will consider giving up work because of their symptoms - 10% will give up work. (Irish and UK statistics)

The above are shocking statistics. We are so poorly educated about this major life event. We wouldn't dream of not preparing ourselves or our teenagers about puberty, would we? Yet, we treat menopause, which is effectively 'puberty in reverse' so differently. There is stigma, shame, embarrassment, and the demise of youth associated with menopause. And we are still an ageist society, sadly.

There are some great resources for women to educate themselves about menopause, but there are also some peddling myths, which makes the topic so confusing. So, women beware!

The Menopause Hub principles are Education, Empathy and Empowerment. Here are my recommendations for information on menopause, I hope it will guide people to find the right data -

Websites:

- The Menopause Hub
- British Menopause Society (BMS)
- Women's Health Concern
- North American Menopause Society (NAMS)
- Menopause Taylor
- The Menopause Doctor

Support Groups online:

The Irish Menopause
Harley Street at Home

In your opinion, what have you found to be the biggest obstacles you have come across with your clients and can you tell us more about your business and your approach?

Henny:

The biggest obstacles we face are generally from ourselves. They can be many and varied and really depend on each individual - but what enables us is a willingness to change. Whether that's changing an old story, an old pattern, belief or behaviour.

Coaching is all about change. And for many of us perimenopause marks a time where things we've suppressed or boxed away in the past can arise. I term it the real Pandora's Box.

It's as though we've been given a box at puberty, and throughout our lives, we've used it to store all the things that were too difficult, complex, painful, time-consuming to deal with.

Then, when we're peri-menopausal, the box lid starts rattling. And we have a choice.

To sit on the lid, as many of the women in our past would have had to do, or we can choose to address what's there, in the way that feels best to us.

Every single one of us holds the capacity and the capability to make the changes we desire.

My approach is to hold space - entirely free from judgement and dogma, so clients can safely explore whatever it is they choose to bring to the session. The art of self-care underpins the work I do - because that creates a solid bedrock - even when the path feels challenging.

I know from my own experience of being coached how powerful working with a trusted other can be... both in the sessions them-selves, and afterwards, as everything percolates. In truth, the time between sessions is part of the process - neurologically, it is when we rest that we change.

Menopause is a time of change and opportunity and the work I do is often at the deeper level, creating deep and lasting change across all aspects of people's lives. I see such beautiful shifts in how people perceive themselves and their situations. It's why I do the work!

Loretta:

The biggest obstacle is the lack of awareness and education about menopause among women and in society in general. My story is a perfect example. Women who attend our clinic (either in person or virtually, via telehealth video) often have no idea what is happening to them, particularly when the infamous hot flushes aren't experienced. Anxiety, depression and fluctuating moods are so common, causing women to think that they are 'going mad'.

And women often think that they cannot have menopausal symp-toms until their periods stop. A myth. Women are very often their own worst enemy, as they do not speak openly about how they are feeling, some embarrassed to discuss it with friends and family.

Another significant obstacle is the lack of supports available. The Menopause Hub is Ireland's only dedicated menopause clinic. At present, we are inundated with enquiries, appointments and are just about keeping pace with demand. Our research tells us that just under half of women in Ireland feel confident about discussing menopause with their GP.

The Menopause Hub is borne out of my own experience. My vision was to have a team and range of services where women feel comfortable, confident and reassured that they are in the right hands. Our range of services include holistic and medical experts, a psychologist, an acupuncturist, a physiotherapist and a dietitian and nutritionist. Women do not need a referral and can book an appointment via our website www.themenopausehub.ie and our email is info@themenopausehub.ie or call us on 01 2107948.

Is there anything good about the menopause?

Henny:

In short, yes! Menopause often comes at a time in our life when we're dealing with other things. Ageing parents, children either leaving the nest or the realisation that our options to have children are reducing; maybe increased challenges at work, either through promotion or feeling restricted by an invisible Menopause Wall (an unconscious bias we often see in organisations) And grief can often play a part too.

Either grief at the loss of a loved one, or grief at lost opportunities or grief at losing our sense of who we were, without knowing who we're yet to become. It's a melee of emotions and situations that can leave us feeling breathless and overwhelmed.

And yet. It's also a wonderful time to take stock. To breathe and see what's happening. To reconnect with ourselves, with who we are now. And make choices about what we want to come next, and how we want to be.

Loretta:

Yes, there are two things, as I see it.

Firstly, no longer having periods is a terrific freedom as is the fear of getting pregnant.

Secondly, menopause is a wake-up call for women to look after their health. In the 1900's the average age of menopause was forty-seven and the average life expectancy of women was forty-nine.

Nowadays, the average life expectancy of women is eighty-three years, and the average age of menopause is fifty-one. So, we are likely to spend one third to one-half of our lives post-menopausal.

The lack of oestrogen impacts our bone health (osteoporosis), our heart health (heart disease – after menopause the incidence of heart disease rises dramatically, overtaking that of men) and cognitive health (Alzheimer's).

Replacing that lost oestrogen is crucial for long term health but few women know that. Some women also talk about a newfound freedom in general. They don't suffer fools gladly, they don't care what others think so much. That may be menopause or just wisdom with age.

What would you like to see changed across the media and in other public arenas to benefit women's health and awareness?

Henny:

More compassion. It's simple really. When we come at things from a position of tension then it creates tension in the response.

We need to bring our practical compassion and wisdom to how we talk about menopause - removing the taboo that still surrounds it and seeing it exactly as it is...A life stage that EVERY woman will experience in her life, and every man will indirectly experience through the women in their lives too. Just like periods, puberty, death, birth and love, menopause is simply a part of life.

Loretta:

I would dearly love to see two things -

1. More high-profile Irish women coming out and talking about their menopause and how they dealt with it. There are a lot of high-profile women in the United Kingdom and the United States who are doing just that and helping to break the taboo of menopause e.g., Michelle Obama, Mariella Frostrup, Meg Matthews, Lis Earle.

2. I would welcome a public awareness campaign that would educate women (and men) about menopause. This would help women understand what is happening to them and help them realise that they are not alone.

And it would empower women to seek help, which would, in turn, drive up the availability of specialist services to meet that demand.

I think that this would be a terrific step in the right direction for awareness and for living your best life.

Finally, I would like to thank both my guests for this interview. Two outlooks and experiences from two inspiring women who are open and honest with their stories on menopause.

SINEAD TYNAN BYRNE

Sharing her incredible journey
with Multiple Sclerosis

Contact:

Instagram: Sinead Tynan Byrne
Email: sineadtynanbyrne@gmail.com

Loretta Whelan - Reiki master/Reflexologist
Website: www.nurturetherapies.ie
Instagram: Loretta Nurture Therapies

*"In May 2013, my life changed forever when
I heard the devastating news that I had Multiple
Sclerosis (MS) I was a thirty-nine-year-old mother
of three and wife to Bernard"*

$\mathcal{C}$an you share how this shocking news affected you and your family?

It was November 2012; I was in St Vincent's Hospital waiting on results of an MRI. I really wasn't expecting what happened next; the doctor called me in, and I sat down.

After a short chat she started turning the monitor around (something must be wrong), it was so frightening. She suggested, I shouldn't worry and not to google anything, but she thought I might have Multiple Sclerosis (MS) and they would know more after more tests.

To say we were devastated is an understatement, I remember that day like it was yesterday. The tests took six months (six months in limbo).

On the 27th of May 2013, I was diagnosed with Relapsing-Remitting Multiple Sclerosis (RRMS). Another day that will be etched in my mind for the rest of my life; my dad and husband both cried that day.

This will give you an insight as to the devastation we were feeling as a family. My feelings turned back to my beautiful children and what type of mother I could be to them if I got extremely sick and would they end up minding me. It was such a sad time; I really could not stop crying. I decided to tell them very early in the diagnosis. They are very bright and knew something was wrong, so myself and Bernard, my husband, told the kids in June. They were brilliant, so kind, caring and helpful around the house, they could not have done enough.

News travels fast and I know people meant well by getting in touch, but I really did not have any time to digest the devasting news and I wasn't coping very well. I decided to go to counselling to talk about how I was feeling. I found it so helpful; I started to make peace with the diagnosis.

I was always googling looking for ways to beat this disease or at least keep it at bay. My head was wrecked trying to help myself. I got in touch with a homeopath and started taking a lot of different supplements and even changed my diet. I was Vegan for a year. It was helping but the fatigue was crippling, and I knew I was slowly losing more and more of myself as time went by. I had to do something. What could I do?

The campaign "Sinead's Stems of Hope" was set up to raise much needed funds to help your journey to better health. How successful was your campaign?

One day I remember sitting in my friend Nicola's car in the carpark at the school and saying to her "NOTHING IS WORKING OUT IN MY LIFE; I DON'T WANT TO END UP IN A WHEELCHAIR FOR THE KIDS WEDDINGS...."

I was holding back the tears when the kids came out, I couldn't let them see me heartbroken. Myself and my friend had been talking about stem cell treatment again. I told her my interest in going to check it out.

I had seen a video of an Australian nurse called Kirsty Cruise, she had

been to Moscow and had brilliant results. So, after months of research, I decided along with my family that I would go. I had hope again, hope of a bright future again.

It was so good to think I had a chance to stop this disease and get my life back. I was also the first Irish woman to go to Russia for this treatment.

The next step was money, it was expensive. Nicola said to me we will have the money by Christmas, and she was right, we did. It was amazing. We set up a campaign called Sinead's Stems of Hope and started fundraising.

Bernard took the lead here and was amazing at organising everything. We had great help from our best friends- Ian, Teri, Derek, Gwen and of course Nicola and our wonderful families. I think people get a lot out of giving and helping, it is like a ripple effect. I really believe what you give out you get back tenfold.

The campaign was so humbling and brought me to tears on more than one occasion. It was an amazing experience, and it changed my life in so many ways; people where so generous and they could not do enough. We organised a Hell and Back, the Women's Mini Marathon, the Dublin City Marathon, a coffee morning, cake sales, golf classics and quizzes. The whole community where fantastic and I felt so proud to have lived here all my life and know so many people who really backed me from the get-go. I will be forever grateful to each and everyone.

Living in a pandemic does not help anyone's mental health... How are you feeling now, and have you completely changed your outlook on life?

During the pandemic I have missed hugs and kisses. I'm dying to give a great big hug to my mam and dad. I look forward to holidays again, meals out with friends, coffees and chats. But the main thing is that we all stay well and safe. f I'm fine with that.

When I think about my mental health, I think about how I was as a child and my mam always said I was happy and good humored. I'm definitely more positive and optimistic than negative. Even when I was sick, I had days where I was just sad, and the darker days didn't last too long. I'm not saying I didn't cower in a corner and feel despair once or twice - I did.

But there was always something to smile about and somebody worse off than me. My kiddies always made me smile and kept me going. Even when I was sick, I felt lucky for all I had and that my disease progression was slow. It's coming up to my fourth-year post stem cell transplant and yes, this treatment has totally changed my life.

That old saying your health is your wealth is so true and for it to be taken away and the devastation, pain, suffering and loss you experience - it's just indescribable. Then for it to be given back to you in the same lifetime, it really makes you appreciate life, health and everything so much more.

It's like winning the lottery. I'm loving life, I'm happy and I don't really worry too much about the small stuff. I feel lucky and grateful. and have a real zest for life again. I'm determined to enjoy and cherish everything that life has to offer. I have a huge admiration for people living with long term illnesses or disability as I've experienced it first-hand. The pain and suffering people experience, nobody will understand it unless they've lived it.

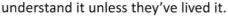

Can you explain to the TLC audience what Hematopoietic Stem Cell Transplantation (HSCT) is and how it saved your life?

Hematopoietic Stem Cell (HSC) transplantation is an intensive chemotherapy for MS. It aims to stop the damage MS causes by wiping out and regrowing your immune system using your stem cells. A treatment that is not available in Ireland now.

It's a fantastic treatment and many people have had amazing results and seen a reverse in symptoms.

If anybody is reading this and has MS, google Kirsty Cruise - 60 minutes Australia to see for themselves.

I arrived in Moscow with Bernard for four weeks; from start to finish we were looked after so well by Dr Fedorenko and his wonderful team. It was not any easy treatment and recovery was extremely difficult, but it was worth it. In the early days of the treatment, you receive testing before you are accepted for the treatment, including chest x rays, heart function and MRI blood tests.

If you are accepted, you start your treatment and receive drugs to stimulate your own bone marrow into your blood stream where its collected and frozen. The next step is receiving intensive chemotherapy to kill your immune system. On your transplantation day your stem cells are reintroduced to your immune system to multiply and graft your new immune system. You must then stay in isolation. I stayed in isolation for eight days only able to look at Bernard through a window or on face time. It was a difficult time looking back on it now.

But I was happy to rest and recover. I meditated every day and it really helped me to focus on the here and now and just allow myself to be. It was during this period I noticed a change in my energy levels, and I started to feel I had more energy, and my cognitive ability was starting to get better, I was remembering things again. I was feeling no pain, I could not believe it was happening so quick.

I had suffered dreadful pain in my left shoulder for years and was delighted this was gone, what an added bonus.

The treatment was life changing in that I have energy again. Less pain, better cognitive ability, and a huge hope that my MS was halted and not living in dread of the future.

Can you share any words or any acts of kindness that you received that helped you during your treatment and recovery?

There are so many moments during the campaign that stands out for me and too many people to mention.

But one act of kindness really touched my heart and changed my life. A friend that went to school with my husband, her name is Loretta Whelan had seen the campaign on Facebook and offered to do reflexology on me to help me relax and unwind.

I didn't know at the time that we would become great friends. It was

really life-changing, she really helped me heal and repair.

I loved and looked forward to my treatments every week. She also did Reiki and Workshops. She was so self-less and so giving and is an incredible healer and life coach.

I loved it so much I decided to go back to college at nighttime and I qualified as a reflexologist myself and I'm also qualified in Reiki level two - both fantastic treatments.

She introduced me to the power of the mind and the ability we have to heal our lives and the ripple effect it can have on everyone around you. It raises your vibration.

I also received anonymous donations and I will never forget that first week when friends called to hand me money, it was so humbling. I'll never forget who they were and often its people that you don't expect. The I love you cake that Karen made for me and the going away party. I found it so hard to hold back the tears before we left for Russia. I will never forget that.

I'll never forget my first Stemmie present a pal sneaked into Bernard's case. All the beautiful good luck and get-well cards, just so many to mention and the keep the faith one-liner from Benny.

All these gestures, I will never forget, they mean so, so much.

ROB CULLEN

Speaker, MC, Coach

Contact:

Twitter: robcullen79
Instagram: Rob and Yvonne

*Y*ou have a fantastic weight loss journey. Can you share some tips on how you maintained your weight loss?

Thanks Yvonne, I think there are a few reasons why we managed to keep the weight off. I'll take you back to the start as I feel this is key to keeping the weight off.

We had a strong motive and a strong why to losing the weight in the first place for us, it was our boys and our health. When you have a strong why you keep going.

It's always there so it's not a short term why like an occasion (birthday/ holiday/wedding) it's something that we could keep going back to and keep reminding ourselves why we started.

The second reason that we have been able to maintain our weight loss is due to how we lost it in the first place.

We made a conscious decision never to be on a diet, to make some small changes and make them sustainable.

So now it's just a way of life for us. We eat and cook healthy most of the time, treat ourselves when we want but really enjoy the food we are cooking and eating.

It's not all plain sailing though but sometimes you need to take a step back and look in the mirror to realise how far you have actually come.

Have some snacks throughout the day but know the difference between a snack and a treat, we try keep our treats for the evening - during the day we would snack mainly on fruit.

With Christmas holiday time coming to an end, what are your suggestions to getting back on track and into a healthy eating plan as soon as possible?

Most of us have overindulged over the last few weeks but the truth is if you do absolutely nothing other than going back to your regular way of eating and moving you will actually lose the weight you might have gained within two to three weeks.

Even we take a break over the Christmas, but we still try to make better choices and that is what it's all about. The first week in January, we go back to our weekly planner of what we are having for dinner each night. We sit down on a Sunday and come up with some ideas on meals we would like to have during the week (remember if you don't feel excited about it on Sunday you won't want to eat it on Wednesday)

We don't make it until that evening, but we know what ingredients we need to have, to make it.

We always try to have plenty of colour, variety and a mixture of quick and easy meals to make. A simple process is to have a quarter of your plate protein, a quarter carbs and half with veg. Watch the portion size too, if you feel you need more, top-up on the veg. Make sure your meals are filling and enjoyable.

We get back to our porridge for breakfast, Yvonne has plenty of different ways of making it and tons of recipes on Instagram. Have some snacks throughout the day but know the difference between a snack and a treat, we try to keep our treats for the evening - during the day we would snack mainly on fruit.

It really is that simple, just make the small sustainable changes, love what you eat, enjoy any sort of exercise you do and this all makes it so much easier to become a daily habit. Motivation will get you started but habits are what keep you going.

What's your opinion on quick fix weight loss programmes and is it sustainable long term?

Quick fixes just don't work, we will see so many false promises and advertisements over the next few weeks about how you could look if you did X but it's all bullshit really. They are not sustainable as people on them are hungry and craving any food groups they might have cut out. Once they go back to 'normal' the weight goes back on.

Slow and steady really does win the race. Nothing that comes easy will last and nothing that lasts comes easy.

In saying that, some are good to get people back on track but don't think if you do something for four weeks in January you are going to win 2021, it has to be consistent.

"It really is important to stay connected,
eighty per cent of success in networking comes
not from meeting new people but from maintaining contact with
your existing network."

A big part of what you do in Dublin Chamber is linked with networking, how have you found virtual networking in 2020 and for the foreseeable future?

Oh, I've really missed face to face networking. 2020 has been a tough year for anyone like me who loves networking and was doing it most days - online is just not the same.

I've tried many different platforms and events over the last ten months now but really it is hard to replicate a face-to-face event. But we are going to have to do it for the next six months at least so I would say, keep networking online and think of the positives,

Our network now is no longer geographically restricted, we can reach out to people, connect and do business globally, when we might not have even considered it last year.

Everyone is available so it's easier to connect and arrange a zoom call with people.

You need to keep relevant, keep sharing content, keep reaching out to people but the key to any networking is helping others.

Don't be a taker be a giver, be that person that helps connect people that helps others do business. The more you give in the long run the more you will get back.

Can you share your new concept of networking introduced in December and was there good feedback from it?

Yes, recently Dublin Chamber launched a new way of networking on a platform called Remo. Think of yourself arriving at a wedding and looking at the table plan, that's what happens when you arrive at our new networking events.

You will see a table plan and hop on a table with up to five other people, you will see them, and they will see you and you network with each other. Every few minutes we encourage people to move onto another table to increase their connections and chat to others.

If we have a guest speaker, the networking stops and people will all see the speaker on the main stage.

We have only tried a couple of events, but the overall feedback has been great, people loved the tables and a small tight group conversation so we will see how it goes in 2021.

Finally, what are your plans for going forward?

I wear many hats so my main goal for 2021 will be to stay healthy, spend as much time as possible with my family and continue to help others.

Whether it's in health and wellbeing, connecting businesspeople with each other or just offering help and advice, there is nothing more satisfying than seeing someone else succeed from the help you have given them.

It is the hardest time of the year to stay motivated and lose weight. Thank you, Rob, for all your tips that will most definitely help people at home.

The main thing is to stay positive and focused on your ideal goals...

LIZ SHEEHAN

Author, Crystal Therapist

Contact:

Website: lizsheehan.ie

$\mathcal{C}$an you share a summary of your career and how you became a Crystal Therapist?

I spent many years working in the fashion industry, starting with A-Wear when I was in school and continuing on to work as a store manager/Merchandiser/ Fashion Buyer for the likes of Brown Thomas and Penney's. I traveled a lot in my twenties, so I supplemented that with working in hospitality and catering.

I also segued into working as the wardrobe manager for an Irish Dance show called Rhythm of the Dance where I was on a world tour for three years. I did some film and panto work and eventually moved back into management for Starbucks. I was working as a store manager and management trainer for Starbucks, where I opened the Malahide branch.

On the birth of my second child, I left to open my own business, Paua2thepeople a handmade crystal jewellery and accessory business.

As I was working for myself, I had the flexibility to work around the kids while they were young. In 2014, we moved to Wicklow, and I took some time out to retrain as a yoga teacher, a reiki master and a crystal healing therapist. I also wrote my first novel - Beneath The Visible.

You have written your first fiction novel "Beneath The Visible" – Can you tell readers what genre it is for and why you write in this style?

It's a fast-paced action fantasy adventure novel for the young teen reader. I was attracted to writing for this age group as primarily this is where my kids sit on the reader demographic. I wanted to open up the world of crystals to them but in a way that wasn't preachy or obviously teaching.

I learned this by teaching kids' yoga and mindfulness. It had to be disguised as anything but yoga.

I think this works in my writing too. The information is gleaned almost by osmosis and hopefully in a fun way.

You have said before that the story just came to you and the characters; you have a creative nature, is this important to you in your daily life also?

I think if you are a creative person then it's vital to express that energy or it stagnates. When I moved to Wicklow first, I joined an art class and I still meet with the people from that class to sketch and draw in our houses or in any of the many fab locations here. I think creativity just oozes out of people if they are that way inclined, but I also believe everyone is creative; just some people think they are not because they couldn't draw in school or didn't get a chance to find a creative expression for themselves.

> *"Creativity is not just about the obvious - art*
> *and writing, it can be how a person arranges*
> *their furniture so that it feels right to them,*
> *or simply how they go about their day"*

We need a broader definition of this, and I am glad to see that the educational system has evolved since I went to secondary. I wasn't allowed to do art. I scored high on the aptitude test and went into the 'A' stream, where languages, science and academics were prioritized.

This led me to study applied science in college and I now have a science degree where I can honestly say I have never used. I did at the time take the leaving cert art exam and I am happy to report got an honor in it, much to the chagrin of the principal at the time but it was too little too late for me to apply to art college.

What have you learned about your business and yourself, this past eighteen months, living through a pandemic?

I think the most important thing I learned is to keep pushing through. I spent most of my time applying for grants for my website and working on that.

The focus of my business also changed as I was a yoga and mindfulness teacher so I had to pivot and focus on my books and other products which will be coming online soon. In any business you need to move with the cheese as they say and being rigid in your thought process, focus or direction won't work if the world goes topsy turvy.

Having a flexible attitude helps. I think if this was a haiku it would be – "Be like water...it flows...." or something to that effect.

Can you share any words of wisdom you received from other people in your life, which you have never forgotten?

I don't know if they are words of wisdom, but I will share a motivator for me - Sean Scully.

Sean Scully is an artist who spent time in the eighties scouting around the art galleries of New York looking for any interest in his art. I watched a documentary where he was telling the story of his life, which was really hard, starting with being homeless as a child on the streets of Inchicore.

Because of this upbringing, when the gallery owners dismissed him, he read this to be, that they were interested as they weren't physically throwing him out on the street. His utter belief in himself and his work propelled him to being one of the most successful artists today.

When the interviewer questioned him on why some gallery owner didn't promote his art, he sat there and questioned the interviewer as to why he would even wonder that.

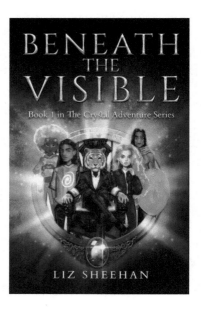

MARGUERITE PENROSE

Anti-Racism Campaigner, Reiki Master, Author

Contact:

Twitter: magsimaloo
Instagram: magsimaloo

*Y*our story is about Adoption, you were born in St Patrick's Mother & Baby Home. Have you ever pursued more information about your early years and why your life began in St. Patricks?

For me, life began in St.Patricks, I presume because my biological parents were not together when I was born. My biological mother knew she couldn't provide for me and my medical needs, amongst other factors.

My biological father although aware of me, must not have been in a position to raise me either; he had returned to his homeland prior to my birth.

Over the last few years, I've explored a bit more into life in St. Patrick's and why my life began there. I've just recently connected with a wonderful woman, Cathy, who worked in St. Patrick's.

She cared for myself and two other children who were in my section of the home during her time working there.

Cathy heard my interview with Ryan Tubridy and contacted the show when I was still on air. Since then, myself, Mum, Dad, and my sister went to visit Cathy and reconnected. Cathy was able to tell me about my life in St. Patrick's for the approximate eighteen months she worked there.

She cared for me and was the first person to bring me outdoors. Yes, can you believe I was only eighteen months old and never been outside, despite the home being on huge grounds.

She sought permission to bring me on day trips at first and was later also permitted to take me home for weekends. For some time, I was loved and cared for by her family too. Cathy was only eighteen years old at the time herself, therefore she was too young to adopt herself. She said she would have liked to have had the option had she been older.

I feel so privileged to have had someone so special who at the age of eighteen, had the kindness to love me and my other friends who were with me in St. Patrick's. It's been over forty-three years since we first met and now an even bigger privilege to know her again and meet her in person.

I was also adopted when I was a baby, which is where we found a mutual connection. I have found trying to trace my birth parents emotionally draining because of the lack of information that can be released to the adopted child, what has your experience been?

To be honest I can't even begin to explain how I feel about tracing biological parents in Ireland. It's a minefield. I've dipped my toe in the water in relation to tracing and going through Tusla. It's such a long emotional process and you can be waiting up to five years to even get a caseworker to be assigned to you.

Don't get me wrong, I know we can be handed pieces of paper with our biological parent's name, address, and phone number, however, why can't the system of tracing be professionally overhauled? Our details are literally in someone's 'filing cabinet' or archived somewhere.

As you know Yvonne, we are not even entitled to our medical history and it's only of late, we can finally get our own birth certificates.

I think this was only permitted in the last few years, prior, it was an 'adopted birth certificate'. I could go on about this topic, it's obviously one close to our hearts and causes great pain when I actually think properly about it. However, I'm glad to say being adopted is a bonus ninety-nine per cent of the time.

"I'm blessed with two sets of parents and ancestors, even if I'll never know my biological side. I know a lot of adopted people feel very angry, frustrated and annoyed at the system and they have every right to be - the system is a shambles"

The more you delve into adoption, the more hidden truths you uncover. I've recently sent off my DNA kit, and I'm anxious about the results. I've only a piece of paper to tell me very limited information about my heritage and who's to say the information is correct?

From hearing other adoptee stories, I know many have learned their heritage is not always as they were told. Naturally, I'm eager to know as much as I can but I am also anxious about the results.

Your Twitter name 'Unapologetically Black' reflects your undeniable passion for change, how have you found social media as a platform for your values and issues?

Over the last few months, I've been actively speaking/ posting about racism and encouraging everyone to be and declare themselves 'Anti-Racist'. I use the words declare yourself Anti-Racist, as sadly, that's what is needed now. It's not good enough to just presume people know you're Anti-Racist.

It's not about Irish, African, American racism- it's about all forms of racism. People don't seem to understand that racism is a huge issue here in Ireland as well as worldwide; an issue like many that shouldn't even exist. Obviously being born in Ireland but having a Zambian (as I've been told) biological Father, colour has always been a part of my life.

I would call myself black, others might not give me that title, as my skin is lighter. But as I say, "It's my skin, therefore my choice.

I honor my heritage and I'm proud to be Black and Irish. So many people unfortunately state that we cannot be classed as Irish, why - because we are not white. For me, it's hurtful and so much more that sometimes words fail me. I was born in Dublin in 1974, I would call myself patriotic but yet others see me as an intruder; someone who doesn't belong.

I am, along with others campaigning (each in our own way) to educate people that Irish is no longer just a white person status. Was it ever? I ask myself when we look back through the years. Many people who travelled, married, and had children here are from every part of the world. So, why is it still not accepted that Black/Brown/Asian born in Ireland are not classed as Irish? (For some people)

I must and want to lend my voice to the campaigns, no matter how small it is in doing something to bring about change.

I should not have to explain who I am, where I'm from and what my passport states to anyone.

Accept me for me, as I accept you for you. But on numerous occasions, I do have to explain and because of this, I'm now speaking out openly. I would always have defended myself and others in the past, it's just now myself and others are using all these platforms to talk about it more.

"I had some negative experiences, the usual name-calling- 'Choc ice', half-caste (this terminology really hits me hard). The 'where are you really from' and the 'but you are not black really"

What needs to be modified to educate people/children, more on this issue?

In my opinion, there is a huge amount of change needed from within the home, workplace, education system, and society in general. I feel part of what I am doing is to ask people to be a voice too; to post educational information and to have uncomfortable conversations about racism with people.

We can all say the wrong thing unintentionally, I am guilty of that too, why? Because I am human.

If people are willing to educate themselves and change, well then, we must be willing to accept their changes. The past is gone, we cannot change it, but we can commit to being better for the future.

I'm not saying forget about the past, I am saying we must use it as another mechanism to make the changes needed for now and future generations. These are changes needed by each and every one of us. We need more education within schools from day one of going to school. Parents need to have conversations with their children about inclusivity and diversity. Every workplace needs to have anti-racism policies, along with its other established policies.

"I experienced racism throughout the years and
when it happened, I had to deal with it and move
on as so many others have had too as well.
All racism is unacceptable"

I feel that a lot of people are telling their stories at the moment, therefore people think we only have a problem with racism now. I have heard statements such as 'we are jumping on the bandwagon' because of what has been happening in America. This isn't the case, racism isn't a bandwagon, this is something that shouldn't even exist.

I can only speak about my own personal experience and why I've always hated that sometimes I had to laugh off racism, due to embarrassment, or fear of causing a scene. I've learned over the past few months that there are also so many people who are in solidarity with us and this is what makes our movement even greater. We are not alone.

What is next for you as an activist and campaigner for anti-racism?

My next and current project is with our charity black tie ball which I announced when speaking on The Ryan Tubridy Show.

This ball is scheduled for next year and is about eliminating racism by bringing everyone together in celebration. Bringing people together no matter what race they are, sex or creed, whilst also shining a spotlight on our chosen charity.

The ball is currently in the preparation stage, and I have a small team of wonderful women currently onboard with me for this event. It will be launched via our website, which I hope to have ready by October/November.

All details will be revealed including the date, time, place, and of course, the chosen charity will be announced. We will welcome all sponsorship offered (so feel free to contact us once launched)

We look forward to a night with a difference, whilst also making a difference. Everything on the night will reflect our mission; it will be a night filled with a diverse selection of talented artists and not forgetting our guest speakers. By being there on the night, sends a clear message that you support that change is needed in Ireland for all generations.

The team and I are putting a huge amount of work into this project as it's the first of its kind in Ireland, born from the Black Lives Matter movement in Ireland. The Black and Irish page on Instagram (where it began) highlighted our stories and gave me my anti-racism platform. It also gave me the ambition and drive to do something constructive for our movement and for others.

Connection is important, and by bringing people together in solidarity for a night of celebration is a big message to one and all.

If I can conclude by thanking everyone including yourself Yvonne, the guys who run the Black and Irish platform, who have given me and others a platform to be heard, and also to family, friends, and many strangers who have supported myself and others on this journey.

"For me the true meaning of life is connection,
when we connect to ourselves, each other
and the universal forces, we become aligned"

Grá

RACHEL THORNBURGH

Sales, Project Management and Entrepreneur

Contact:

LinkedIn: Rachel Thornburgh
Instagram: re_jingled

*"Through a series of unexpected, life altering events,
I found myself embarking on a post grad in UCD.
My name is Rachel, and I am a forty-year-old
student" (extract from an article you wrote
in the College Tribune)*

Can you share what the unexpected, life altering events were and if going to college was a positive direction for you?

I held a post for fourteen years, which I loved. It was full of variety; it challenged me and was incredibly rewarding. Over the years, various interested parties had approached the company that I worked for wanting to buy the building. It's quite special. A Gothic Victorian edifice located in central Dublin.

Eventually, the company decided to sell and sold it a lot quicker than any of us expected, which ultimately led to my redundancy. It left me feeling quite out of sorts and I struggled for the first couple of months.

Apart from looking for a job and trying to navigate the social welfare system, which I thought I'd be amazing at, I was terrible.

A friend, who was in a similar position, had just completed a Diploma in the Innovation Academy in University College Dublin (UCD) via Springboard. She nudged me towards their website, and I perused the course listings. I found a Post Grad Certificate in Creativity, Innovation and Entrepreneurship that was accepting applications for their February admissions. I applied and was fortunate enough to be accepted. Apparently, they can only cater to four per cent of their applicants, although I'm sure that has since changed as they have since become entirely virtual.

Returning to college was exciting and disquieting all at once. On my first day, I managed to not succeed at public transport, became lost and disorientated... twice. Belfield is an abyss and one that I had never encountered. I was nervous too, as I knew that the course work entailed a lot of project group work and multiple, impromptu presentations. Presentations, my biggest abhorrence, however I knew that I had been bestowed with a wonderful opportunity and magic certainly does happen when one steps out of one's comfort zone, so I went at it hell for leather.

During my first week, I had approached the College Tribune and, following my experience of day one, asked them if they wanted a piece on 'Returning to College in your 40s'. I sent the editor a draft. He liked it. It resulted in me contributing an additional five articles to the newspaper, completely and entirely based on my college experience whilst raising and organising a family, coming to terms with being unemployed and juggling home school. Oh, and did I mention the pandemic?

All in all, college was a super experience, I catapulted myself into it, and sometimes my kids were there in the virtual classroom with me. Surprisingly and entirely unexpectedly, of three awards available, I was on the winning team for a project award and winner of our final project award. Both awards were voted for by my peers. I'm moved every time I think about that.

"I didn't even know what Zoom was back in March,
but it quickly became my new best friend"

Can you tell the TLC audience about Re-Jingled, your business venture?

Re-Jingled has been in the background for several years. Re-jingling is the process of reusing and repurposing unwanted fabrics in the production of children's sleepwear, occasion wear and accessories.

The philosophy behind Re-Jingled is to promote environmental friendliness in an effort to combat fast fashion and to produce unique items of children's clothing.

Each item produced tells its own story with a brief description of where the fabric came from and its previous life.

Everything is handmade and each item is one of a kind. I am self-taught sewist and have always been creative. My mother was a seamstress alongside her day job, but I was never allowed near her industrial Novum, until she gave it to me after doing a big clear out.

With my trusty friend YouTube, I learned some simple techniques and I started making things like straightforward envelope style cushion covers. As a beginner, I was eager to learn more but didn't have the cash to fork out on fabrics and so I began using what was already around the house. As I grew more confident, I made my daughter a pair of kimono style pyjamas from a beautiful duvet cover with china dolls all over it.

I sourced it from my local Vincent's charity shop as I still wasn't quite courageous enough to potentially mess up new fabric. Re-Jingled moved on from there. I have since done some research on fast fashion and its impact on the environment and it's simply mind blowing and saddening. From working conditions to water waste and pollution and even as far as recycling practices - clothes production wreaks havoc on our environment.

Re-cycling is great but what's greater is to reuse. So, Re-Jingled is not only about making new from old but it's also about creating awareness, in a fun, 'non preachy' way.

How have you managed personally and professionally throughout the lockdown and the ongoing pandemic?

I found the lockdown somewhat novel initially. That has since evolved. I was really enjoying my time in UCD and so was disappointed that we all had to go home and pick it back up virtually. Not only was it a time for learning again but it was also time for me and suddenly we were all at home toiling with dodgy WIFI, fighting over desk space, overheating devices and home schooling. It was super challenging.

I didn't even know what Zoom was back in March, but it quickly became my new best friend. Having said that, the pandemic opened up an opportunity for Re-Jingled to create face masks from reclaimed fabrics and so I began with those and really started embracing my Instagram account to promote Re-Jingled.

Re-Jingled is like a third child to me, however it doesn't pay the bills, so since finishing up in UCD, I have been focusing on securing employment. I enjoy working and collaborating with a team and quite frankly, I miss the camaraderie.

I've participated in a number of virtual career fairs and carried out ample research on how to perform in a virtual interview. It's also quite possibly the worst time to be looking for employment but necessary, nonetheless. With the pandemic has brought a profound sense of self-awareness. I have good days and bad days but seek gratitude and joy in the daily things.

You have a creative side and say that you "build community around shared interests and goals by bringing ideas to fruition" - How do you achieve this, what are your tools?

One of my primary roles in my previous job was to explore the needs of our internal stakeholders, reach out to external stakeholders and essentially join the dots. It was a dynamic, fluid and collaborative networking exercise which was constantly ongoing. It was satisfying, rewarding and fun. The same applies to my volunteer role as marketing lead in my daughter's school.

A number of parents from different classes assemble regularly and brainstorm ideas. I assist with nourishing those ideas and encouraging ownership.

I don't have any specific tools; however, my mantra is that no idea is a bad idea and I remind myself that when I reach out to someone, the very worst they can say is no, and that's really not that bad.

Can you share any words of wisdom that helped you in your successful career?

Well, I collected many over the years, all of which were warmly received. They not only apply for career but also in the day to day.

Here are some of my favourites:

- Listening is sometimes the best way to help someone.
- Step out of your comfort zone, that's where the magic happens and really what's the worst that could happen?
- Stop caring what other people think, just go for it, get it done.
- Treat others as you would like to be treated.
- Don't dismiss advice from your parents, they have your best interests at heart and have lived.

CIAIRÍN DE BUIS

Former CEO of Women for Election,
a not-for-profit organization

Contact:

Twitter: Ciairín

*C*ould you share a summary of your career to date that has led you to your current position as CEO at Women for Election?

Like many, I've had a career that has wended its way, rather than gone in straight lines.

As you say I currently head up Women for Election an organisation that inspires, equips, and supports women to succeed in politics. Before coming to Women for Election, my focus was on children's rights and early years in particular. I headed up Start Strong, an advocacy organisation focused on children's early years and bringing about change in government policy. After that I did some consultancy work before coming to Women for Election.

Previously I've managed services for people with disabilities, worked as a policy officer, had a brief stint in the civil service and done some work in prisons. I've also served on the Parole Board. As I said, my career hasn't been in straight lines so far!

I've always tended to do voluntary work, outside of the day job, and have had the chance to work with some great groups. I've recently joined the board of the Children's Rights Alliance and am also on the board of Sonas (Freedom from Domestic Violence)

Who are your biggest influencers/thinkers that have helped you build your own strong values in strategic thinking?

Where to start? There's been a lot.

In my family life, it would be my grandmother. She was widowed very young, went back into the workplace (at a time when very few women worked) and brought up her young family. She was adventurous, always on the go, and a force of nature.

Norah Gibbons, who died recently, has been a huge influence in my career over the past decade or so. She was a fearless advocate, a brilliant policy mind, a great mentor and a wonderful friend. I, along with countless others, miss her enormously.

I've been lucky enough to work with a lot of really brilliant people who were very generous in sharing their expertise, experience, talent and skills - mentors, formal and informal, are a key part of the way I work.

We have also found the fundraising environment a real challenge. Over half our annual budget is through fundraising, and our fundraising dinners have had to be canceled – we haven't yet worked out how to fully replace that aspect of our income, but we will get there.

How do you think our accustomed way of life will change in the future and how has Women for Election managed throughout this crisis?

In Women for Election, we've pivoted to online delivery, along with the rest of the world we've been learning about Zoom and other platforms and are working to ensure we still reach as many as we can with our online training and webinars.

We've found we've been able to reach more women, particularly outside of Dublin, and women with whom we haven't worked with before, which is great.

One of the challenges has been, and this is the same for everyone delivering services online, the digital divide. So, for homes without Wi-Fi, or devices, or the space to sit for an hour or two attending a session, our training might be harder to reach than before. That's one we're still figuring out how to tackle.

How will things change in the future? I don't think anyone really knows yet. At least not fully. I think for many of us this Covid Crisis has helped us clarify our priorities in life a bit more – I think working from home will become more normal. I hope we will all value our neighbours and local communities more.

And I hope, we will see a lot more women entering politics – while I think we have seen some brilliant leadership from the Irish political system, we've also seen the real gaps that have happened because there weren't enough women in the room.

Can you share any words of wisdom that you received that helped you in your successful career?

Be ambitious, be audacious, ask questions and remember the why

- Why are you doing this?

SEÁN KELLY

Author, Scriptwriter, Performer

Contact:

Website: www.seanbernardkelly.com
Twitter: @sbernardkelly

W here did your love of writing begin?

I grew up in an era where conversation and reading were the main source of entertainment, as was Radio Eireann. Television had not reached Ireland, yet. As a youngster, comic books were the only reading material and then later adventure novels would have been my cuppa!

The opportunities for creative writing were very limited unless you studied literature or went into journalism. I've had no professional training or grinds in this and am basically 'winging-it'.

During my teens, our local Youth Club was an opportunity to try out something original, especially at talent competitions and our yearly Christmas concerts.

This presented the offering of writing comedy sketches and parodies. Later, I joined various theatrical groups that participated in 'Tops-Of-The Town' which was a huge event sponsored by Player-Wills. Again, comedy scripts and parodies were my preference.

Much later, I was part of the 'Tramore Variety Group' who were the first community group to reach the National Finals (televised live from the Gaiety Theatre in Dublin)

Tobacco advertising or anything related to such, killed-off that competition and all troupes needed sponsorship to present a quality show - Yes, it costs! And the competition died.

I then began writing to the National Press letters page - Always short, sarky , humorous pokes at political events or about the plastic celebs who had managed to get both feet into their mouth with some crazy statement - It was cannon-fodder for me.

I was a founding member of Tramore Writers Group but still never had the urge to attempt anything of a serious piece - my contributions were always of the humorous variety. That was until, I decided to 'have-a-go'.

The result was - "The Dog Sit Affair."

Isolation is part of what writers need to create and think. How has the pandemic affected you both personally and as a writer?

This pandemic probably presented the 'time-zone' for painters, writers and songwriters to exercise their creative juices. Anyone attempting a novel will tell you that they need the quiet and the time, to let their minds cut loose and to just write and write.

Luckily, our family business is an essential profession, so my staff were not affected, and I still needed to oversee things. I really feel so sorry for the small, part time musicians and the arts industry who have been grounded during this pandemic.

Many may never again get a chance to express the gift they were given. I recall a saying -" The artist is nothing without the 'gift', but the 'gift' is nothing without the artist."

I get annoyed listening to some of the well-paid professionals (who have made fortunes over the years) complaining about being neglected in these trying times! Think of all the less known individuals who do it for pittance and purely for the love of it.

Do you create characters with other people in mind that you have met or known?

The characters are total fiction, but I drew on my many years of being self-employed and socialising to 'adapt' some of their quirks! It's also about giving the reader a 'hint' of the individual and allowing them to visualise the scenery and settings themselves and not have everything dished-up in flowery sentences. Allowing them the opportunity to become immersed in the story itself.

Can you share any words of wisdom you received from other people in your life, which you have never forgotten?

A wise man once said, "What this Country needs, is someone who knows what this Country needs."

Don't take rejection letters personally - It's only one person's idea of your hard-work on that particular day.

Another piece of advice was "Mind your own business, and maybe one day, you will have a business of your own to mind" I did. And I have.

Will there be a Dog Sit Affair Two?

I am presently halfway through a second novel (not "Doggie" mark two) It's a similar quirky conundrum of twists and turns, mystery, mixed with a large splash of humor. Being totally honest with you Yvonne, I have no pretensions of being the next big 'thing' in Irish literature.

I enjoy my writing and I genuinely hope the readers can relate to the characters and plots that I've presented and when they've reached the last page, they will say, "I enjoyed that."

I am also contemplating writing a comedy novel, based on scripts I had intended putting on stage prior to Covid. I'm a little unsure how it will transfer, but I will be giving it a shot.

KEITH KELLY

Mental Health Campaigner & Founder of
#JumpersforGoalposts

Contact:

Website: www.jumpersforgoalposts.ie

Facebook: Jumpers for Goalposts

I wanted to highlight more awareness on men's mental health. You have overcome a lot of traumas in your life and come out the other end. Can you share your story?

I suppose looking back, things started to go wrong for me as far back as 2006 when a neighbour began a series of incidents out of the blue that would impact hugely on my mental health. We had always got on and never had bad words between each other.

Over the next two years he continuously did all manner of strange things to torment me and my family.

I tried many times to mediate with him and his family, but it fell on deaf ears.

I also made at least 10/12 complaints to the Garda always attempting to go through the appropriate channels to get to the bottom of the problem but to no avail.

"It culminated in Jan 2008 at 5am with him breaking into my home by throwing my garden bench through the front window and entering my house with a knife. It resulted in me being stabbed numerous times - missing the main artery to my heart by millimetres and puncturing my lungs"

After spending some time in hospital where they were able to patch up my physical wounds, It was my mental health that began to deteriorate. Over the next five years whilst hiding it as best I could from everyone - my life had become unbearable.

I attended some counselling, but I was unable to absorb anything at all from it; I felt a complete failure. My internal dialogue and conversations I was having with myself has constantly been put down by my inner critics- my inner demons.

The side effects included my inability to protect my family home, nightmares, flashbacks, carrying shame (which I now know wasn't mine to carry) anger, rage and revenge.

I had a huge fear of the dark, I was isolating unable to communicate, afraid to show anyone how vulnerable I had become - I was suffering with PTSD (Post Traumatic Stress Disorder).

Trauma is a personal thing and when ignored unfortunately those silent screams continue internally, heard only by the one held captive by that trauma. I always tried to maintain a sense of normality to those around me and looking back now - I was just surviving, not healing.

I was living in a state of fight or flight all the time, with a heightened sense of awareness, always on edge as if awaiting to be attacked at any time.

Gambling, alcohol and drugs became my escape from that pain. When you are suffering with PTSD you become a huge risk taker because you have lost all respect for life. I hated myself, it all just wore me down, I felt I was just a burden to others.

"In 2013, I tried to end all that pain by overdosing."

Thankfully, I wasn't successful. Eventually speaking to my doctor and family, I decided to go back to counselling. My self-esteem and confidence were shattered but I was encouraged to try some voluntary work. A charity called Suicide or Survive (SOS) gave me the opportunity to start rebuilding myself with the help of some wonderful people.

Over the next few years, I went on many self-development courses, wellbeing workshops, wellness programmes and facilitator training courses.

Going to events, enabled me to meet so many people along the way who have struggled with their mental health and have overcome many challenges but are now able to live very productive lives. My creativity, confidence and self-esteem came back, and I was at last able to understand that for me isolation was not where I was gonna heal.

It was in the community of people that I would begin to thrive.

I went back to education and studied counselling skills in Maynooth University, also completing the Train the Trainer Facilitation course with Mental Health Ireland. I am now a fully qualified facilitator in delivering WRAP (a mental health programme) in communities, prisons and other services around the country.

Do I still have tough days? The answer to that would be YES but I now have the tools to navigate my way back to a place of wellness much quicker than before. It's taken an awful long time to get to where I am in life now and I have found out so much about myself.

We all have mental health but maybe we tend to push it to one side until we're really struggling. We need to take great care of our mental health just like we take care of our dental health (we brush our teeth daily, so they don't decay) We need to think of our mental health in the same way.

What I have learned, and I can only speak from my own experience (because there is no one way) is that for me talking really helps, people can and do recover every single day.

J4G gives men an opportunity to leave the ego behind, come together to share a story or two, check in on how life is going on for each other and certainly share some much-needed laughter.

How do you think men's mental health is portrayed in the media and is there enough awareness now compared to ten years ago?

I still think we can do so much more; in the past number of years, I have travelled the country going to recovery colleges. Advanced Recovery Ireland (ARI) is where people from different services come together to share information and stories. Unfortunately, there is a severe lack of funding in Ireland in the mental health sector.

Yes, there is lots more exposure around awareness and while there has been huge progress over the past ten years - the stigma surrounding mental health still needs to be addressed.

I would love to see schools bring wellness/ mental health programmes in as part of the curriculum at the secondary level.

Your initiative 'Jumpers for Goalposts' (J4G) has been such a success; it shows how a simple idea can be so effective. Can you tell us more about J4G?

J4G's success stemmed from a poem I wrote in 2017 called No More Jumpers Thrown Down which went viral and has been viewed over 700,000 times across social media platforms.

It's about me reminiscing about my youth. About how we would leave the house early of a Summers morning, get a ball in a field, throw some jumpers down as goalposts and play for hours on end.

Throughout the day lads would arrive and just join in, that was how we spent our day, often missing dinners and arriving home long after the streetlights had come on.

"The positivity surrounding J4G has surprised us all, but it's become our tribe, our community"

Following on from the poem's success, I received many messages from around the globe from people recalling their own days of playing J4G. From this response, I decided to put out an invitation on Facebook to see if men 18 years and older were interested in an old school game of ball.

There was lots of positivity surrounding my post, so I set a date/time for the following week and over 50 people turned up. We had a great evening full of laughter, misplaced passes, and plenty of shots off target but it was so simple and those who couldn't make it asked when the next game was on.

It has now travelled to many different counties, and we even played a game at Tallaght stadium in front of 6,500 fans on a European night for Shamrock Rovers. J4G gives men an opportunity to leave the ego behind, come together to share a story or two, check in on how life is going on for each other and certainly share some much-needed laughter.

It's a way to make a real connection with fellow men, start that conversation and if we can signpost anyone who is struggling in the right direction- that's what we can do. I have had great support from Michael Nolan, Graham Merrigan and Mark Merrrigan. J4G has been given a platform to talk about men's mental health on The Ryan Tubridy show and other radio stations, along with many national newspapers.

We have had around 1,600 men out playing J4G under the banner of men's mental health, raising awareness and funds for charity Suicide or Survive. It has been a great way to bring communities together; it's totally non-competitive and always ends with the next goal is the winner. We have a J4G Facebook page and a website with all sorts of brilliant videos from games, interviews with ex professionals.

We also did a Christmas special with legends from the past which can be seen on the website.

The interest has been phenomenal with Irish Internationals Richie Sadlier, Keith Fahy playing with us down the end field. Additional participants have included Paul Howard, Eoin Mc Devitt, Pat Flynn and many more ex LOI stars turning up and having a game.

How have you managed during the pandemic, in particular the beginning, when restrictions were extreme and how do you think 'Jumpers for Goalposts' will survive with all the restrictions still in place?

I've managed just fine during the pandemic, there have been days when I might have a sense of frustration and there's been days when I have felt fed up. I am lucky to be living beside Killiney beach and Killiney hill so I always get out with my dog for a stroll on a daily basis.

I find sitting in nature great for the head, I read a lot now, listen to some great podcasts and also do lots of journaling. There was a time in my life when I didn't appreciate nature or just sitting easy.

We had huge plans for J4G that would've happened in June and Covid-19 destroyed those plans but there are far more devastating things going on for others, so many lives lost- businesses gone. We are going to see some tough times ahead and we feel J4G will certainly be welcomed back when restrictions are lifted because communities will find great healing in coming together.

Covid-19 has forced us as people to shut down socially and to avoid any real type of social contact we are used to. I think the longer we feel that sense of disconnection the tougher it can be to reverse that. We need to show a lot of compassion to others and plenty of reassurance that it'll be ok to step outside.

> *"J4G can create that safe, fun, environment*
> *and we will come back stronger than before*
> *- it's the simple things in life that make*
> *such a vast difference in people's lives"*

Meeting up for a chat, laughing together over something silly, kicking a ball about with old mates and not being judged because of the level of one's ability. Sharing an aul tale or two, making a connection on a human level and being part of a tribe were people value you - J4G gives you all the above and more.

In your opinion, is there more that could be applied around mental health, what would you like to see modified or introduced?

There are always improvements that can be made around mental health. I believe for me and the J4G community, it's about spreading awareness and to share our own experiences.

We need to live in a society where people are comfortable enough to share when they feel vulnerable - without being judged.Are there enough services available – NO. How can we change this?

By coming together and becoming community activists, advocating for the changes we want to see at a community level first because that's where we live.

That's where our focus should be and if we can do that through J4G and also put a smile on people's faces - Well everyone's a winner in my book.

BILLY KILKENNY

Dublin City FM Radio Host, Entertainer and Tenor

Contact:

Twitter: BillyKilkenny
Instagram: billykilkenny

*"I host the Good Morning Show on Dublin City FM,
I am a contributor on various today FM shows,
most recently the Mario Rosenstock Sunday roast
and I'm still grafting out a more secure radio career
as we speak - I recently won the Q102 Radio
star search 2020"*

**our radio career only began in 2018, have you found your
dream vocation now?**

Short and simple answer -Yes. I have had many different career paths throughout my twenties and into my early thirties. I started training as a classical tenor and was lucky to sing around the world for various Irish production shows.

Entertainment has always been the theme of any roles I gravitate to and radio ticks every box for me personally and professionally.

When I was sixteen, I selected Ballyfermot Radio School for my work experience which I absolutely loved. Through my touring years when it came to promoting the shows in various countries, I would jump at the chance to do the radio interviews.

The pursuit of my radio career started in 2018 however my dreams of working in radio started many years ago – a dream that's gradually becoming a reality.

Let's talk about singing; you trained as a classic tenor for three years. Would you tell us about this aspect of your career, about Dolly Parton?

After school I wanted to do something with music however, I didn't want four years of academic learning, I wanted something performance based. I was delighted to be accepted into the Conservatory of Music D.I.T in Rathmines where I studied to be a classical tenor. During that time, I worked with the best opera companies in Ireland which were Opera Ireland, Anna Livia Opera and Lyric opera.

This was a great way to earn some money through college whilst gaining stage experience. I was in my twenties, and I wanted to travel so I auditioned to become one of the 'Young Irish Tenors' with an Irish production show called Rhythm of the Dance. All at once, I was on a flight to do a global tour for the next eight months which continued for the next ten years.

"The highlight of my touring days came
when our tour manager told us that we landed
a residency in Dolly Parton's theme park Dollywood
in Tennessee for three months"

When we arrived Dolly's manager asked to see the three tenors. He told us that Dolly had requested to sing with us for the opening show and the opening of her summer season in Dollywood.

Myself and the two other singers Cormac and Tim were gob smacked and found ourselves rehearsing with Dolly Parton singing "When Irish Eyes are Smiling'. She was so kind and genuine and felt like she was really listening to you when you chatted with her.

High on life, the three of us opened the show on our own on stage where I had the pleasure of introducing - "Ladies and Gentlemen...

Dolly Parton..." The audience erupted and Dolly's singing echoed over the three of us. This was our standout moment on tour.

Like myself, you are drawn to human interest stories and your series is aptly called H.I.S. (Human Interest Stories) What gravitates you to this type of reporting?

Growing up I only ever read biographies and life stories, never fiction. I always had a big interest in history and people's lives, so I wanted to incorporate that interest into a programme series on Dublin City FM. I was delighted that the Programme Director took it on and the series that started out as thirteen episodes finished last week, forty episodes later.

Like yourself Yvonne, it's not celebrity life stories that capture my imagination it's the incredible human stories of ordinary people surviving extraordinary situations. I always found inspiration from people's life stories.

I have had guests chat to me about bankruptcy, mental health issues, career changes, surviving illnesses, grief and it always amazes me how resilient human beings are when confronted with major challenges.

I now present The Good Morning Dublin show every Wednesday morning on Dublin City FM and while it's a different format, it still gives me the opportunity to continue interviewing amazing people with fascinating stories.

You have an entertainment trait for sure, where does that creative quality in you come from?

I'm the youngest of four children so I suppose getting noticed was rule number one since I was born. I grew up in a very busy household. My eldest brother was ten years older than me and I've two older sisters in the middle.

My grandmother also lived with us and our family dog Kenny, it was a lively house, so I probably had to shout the loudest. My father would sing and play the guitar at every possible family gathering or party and my mum was always - 'Hostess of the Mostess'.

She would also tinkle on the piano which encouraged me to sing. My brother also plays the guitar so there must be an entertainment gene in us all.

Can you share any words of wisdom that helped you in your successful career?

If it seems a bit scary – go for it!

What I have learned from my experience is that when you're nervous but a little excited about a position or role then that's a great sign. It means deep down you want it.

Jobs may not always go your way, and everyone learns about rejection. I would always encourage people to step a little bit out of their comfort zone as the benefits will stand to you as you move forward with your career.

Each step outside of your comfort zone broadens your horizons and things you would never have contemplated three years ago, end up being your new normal today. So, push yourself for bigger and better opportunities that suit you.

SHARON TREGENZA

Multi-Award-Winning Children's Author

Contact:

Facebook: Sharon Tregenza
Website: www.sharontregenza.com

*W*hat brought you down the path of children's fiction and is there a particular reason you chose to write for this genre?

While living in the Middle East I met the editor of the children's magazine for a large newspaper group. She asked for a "read-aloud story" and I ended up working freelance for them, writing children's and adult content, for almost twelve years.

I wrote a column on how to write poetry for kids, a weekly bedtime story and a series of "strange but true" articles. I did book reviews and the odd short story for the adult magazine too. It was great training on how to write to a brief and keep to a strict deadline.

I secretly enjoyed the children's work more, so when the magazine folded - writing books for children seemed the logical next step.

My first book was set on the Shetland Islands, and I entered it into an international competition.

It won. I was hooked.

You have lived in various parts of the world; do you have a sense of wanderlust still or have you settled down for now?

I thoroughly enjoyed living in different countries and experiencing different cultures but as I've got older, I feel I need my family closer.

I will probably stay in the Bath area but not sure that there won't be another house move.

I'm lucky – I live in a lovely, converted chapel on the top of a hill at the moment and I'm happy here, but who knows....

I was born and brought up in Cornwall so there's always a tug of the heart when I visit relatives there. It's still my favourite county, but the downside is that it's so far from everywhere else and I enjoy seeing my grown children and grandchildren as often as possible.

In relation to creating characters, a previous guest Muriel Bolger spoke

about the array of characters she met while travelling. Did you develop characters from your travels too?

Yes and no.

Most of my characters come from several sources. I may take a physical characteristic from one person and mix it with personality traits from another and then I'll add on some purely fictional bits. Creating characters is great fun. I do use places and events though. I lived in Pembrokeshire and three of my books are set there.

As I said, I grew up in Cornwall and I've recently started work on a series of children's mysteries and the setting is based on Mousehole, a small fishing village near Penzance, where I lived.

Cornish culture is full of mystery and magic – perfect for children's books and who can resist the lure of secret coves and caves. I never could.

As a writer, have you 'enjoyed' the isolation throughout the pandemic and has the time at home made you more prolific?

I must admit I quite enjoyed the lockdown. If someone had said at the beginning of the year, you'll spend three months alone in your house – I would have been horrified.

But as I'm lucky enough to live in a lovely space, I found it very calming. Technology helped too, being in regular contact with family and friends through Zoom and FaceTime etc. made a massive difference.

As for being more prolific? I'd love to say yes, but I haven't been really. I did use the time to catch up on reading through, also watching films and listening to radio plays and I got some writing done.

It also gave me time to work out ideas and plots for new books in my head. An essential part of the writing process.

*"Cornish culture is full of mystery and magic –
perfect for children's books and who can resist the lure
of secret coves and caves. I never could"*

Can you share any words of wisdom that helped you in your successful career?

I think this is best answered by giving you two of my favourite author quotes. I have them blue-tacked to my wall. They've followed me from country to country and county to county and they're as true and relevant today as ever…

"When your story is ready for rewrite, cut it to the bone. Get rid of every ounce of excess fat. This is going to hurt; revising a story down to the bare essentials is always a little like murdering children, but it must be done." — Stephen King And the very pragmatic…

*"A professional writer is an amateur who didn't quit."
— Richard Bach*

RACHEL GOTTO

Author, Clinical Hypnotherapist, Transformational Coach, Speaker

Contact:

Website: www.rachelgotto.com
Facebook: rachelgotto

*C*an we start with your current profession and what its main elements are, and can you share your unusual and powerful life story with the TLC audience?

I work as a personal success coach; a clinical hypnotherapist and I have just completed my memoir and it will be published in 2021.

I am also forming another part of my business as a corporate, motivational speaker. I have an amazing life story and is something I love to share because when I was going through and experiencing multiple traumas, there wasn't very much support, in the sense, we didn't have leaders or people who had been through traumas talking about it.

I remember one really dark time, where I felt truly alone with my experiences, I had complex PTSD, I had experienced multiple losses, sudden death and I had lost my own physicality and my mind.

I wanted to share my story in my memoir and to show people that anything is possible, and we can overcome any obstacle, any challenge providing we follow a few steps and that we understand we ultimately have a choice, and the human spirit is stronger than we think.

We arrived on a boat from England and that in itself is an unusual beginning. I had an adverse childhood that was challenging and that already took away my foundations, so I was always surviving emotionally. My gorgeous brother Dominic got cancer very young, and we were very emotionally co-dependent, and I traveled the world with him trying to find a cure for his cancer and unfortunately to no avail. Sadly, he died with me beside him at the age of twenty-eight, I was twenty-six.

At the age of twenty-three, I started my own business, I was an entrepreneur at a very young age. I was incredibly driven, capable, energetic and at the same time, I was dealing with a lot of emotional issues. When Dominic left, part of me left with him, I was quite destroyed and incredibly bereft.

At the same time, I also met my future husband, which was a great advent into my life, there was a dichotomy of deep, deep loss, and guilt. I felt a survivor's guilt, that it should have been me, I felt I was stronger than Dominic and perhaps, if I had got cancer, I would have survived it. That guilt and falling in love were so difficult for me. A year after Dominic died, I married Nic, and we were incredibly happy. He was a wonderful man, and I was pregnant soon after we married, we had been together for four years.

Nick died eight months later in a scuba diving accident at which I was present. I was six months pregnant and as you can imagine,

I was absolutely devastated after these traumas, and this was the beginning or continuation of PTSD, which I knew nothing about back then. Our daughter, Nicola, was born three months later, and the circumstances of giving birth after such loss were not easy.

That was, of course, another challenging event, Nicola lost the sight in one of her eyes, due to a birthmark. When Nicola was five, she found me unconscious on the kitchen floor. I had a benign, inoperable brain tumor that was growing, and I was unlikely to live beyond two years and I was told I should put my affairs in order, write my will and have Nicola looked after as things were not good.

Not one to lay down and give up, I searched as did my family for someone who could give me a chance of continuing my life. After a long search and a lot of closed doors, I was introduced to a surgeon called Richard Nelson at the Frenchay Hospital in Bristol. He told me if I did survive the operation, I would more or less be paralyzed down the left-hand side of my body, for the rest of my days. I didn't have to think hard about my answer, I had preparatory surgery in London beforehand, incidentally, the operation was not available in Ireland, there was no capacity for it here.

"On January sixth, 2006, I survived a fifteen-hour operation but only just. I had an intracranial bleed in my head, very sick and it was many days after before I moved. I was also paralyzed down the left-hand side of my body"

This was another journey, I had to learn to live with paralysis, being dependent and I refused to accept the prognosis that I would be in a wheelchair for the rest of my life. I fought and fought to the point where I was able to walk. It was many years before my left arm moved at all. It was a long journey and a journey of serious strife but one I was willing to overcome.

I was beginning to feel well but the quality of my life was going downhill rapidly, I was living in a twilight zone.

A very, grey monotone, the only range of emotions I had was rage and anger and deep depression. None of the subtler emotions were available to me! had been put on a lot of medication following surgery as I had intractable epilepsy as a result of the scarring on my brain.

I had been seizing up to twelve times a day, so they had to keep adding in more medication to try to stop the seizures.

Eventually, unaware to me, one of these medications was a Benzodiazepine, and the quality of my life was deteriorating because you need more and more of this drug to stay at the same level you are at. I was in constant intolerance withdrawal. What that meant was, I needed more drugs to feel stable.

I was slowly losing my grip on life, living a twilight life, sleeping during the day, just about managing been a parent, drinking a lot, and just about staying alive. It was only when I found out what Benzodiazepine was, I had to undertake a long journey of withdrawal and it took me two and a half years.

I chartered up forty-seven symptoms I lived with, in those two and a half years. Some of the symptoms included my teeth constantly bleeding, my skin falling off my body, absolute insomnia, Akathisia, I was completely agoraphobic, unable to feel any emotions, and I couldn't even cope with washing up.

> *"Eventually, I became suicidal and homicidal,*
> *and it was a very tough battle to fight those demons,*
> *it was like my mind had become completely dark,*
> *fighting between good and evil. My mind turned against me, so*
> *that is part of the story, and*
> *it is a difficult and dark part of the story"*

It's a very necessary part of this story as there are many people who are the accidental addicts. Society doesn't even see because people don't understand that they are physically dependent on these drugs and it's not possible to just go cold turkey off them.

My story from 2013 to now, has been one of great changes, great movement forward, and great transformations.

I became interested in hypnosis, therapy, and public speaking because I finally realised, that my journey was quite unique, and I had a message that I needed to share with the world.

And that is that we are resilient, we have strength, we just need to choose to tap into our strengths and that we are very powerful as human beings.

I bring all my experiences, all my life skills to the table with each client in a unique, powerful, and transformative way.

When I share my story to a wider audience, It shares wonderful, inspirational messages in it, that people can take with them to understand that they are capable of transformation in their own lives. And that consciousness and choice are vital for us to bring into our lives and to know, we ultimately have choices.

*"The transformations that happen, have
a cascade effect, they affect all areas of your life,
even though you're working on one final point-
so it's very exciting"*

Can you chat more about your statement here, what kind of transformations?

Absolutely! When we positively affect change in one area of our lives, we automatically positively alter another part. I frequently get feedback from clients that the issue we worked on is completely transformed but so is another issue we didn't even look at.

I remember a few years ago, I worked with a lady who completely transformed her fear of speaking in leadership meetings.

When we removed the root cause of her problem, she really began to look forward to her monthly meetings. She became very proficient at speaking and went on to get a promotion because of her newfound confidence.

When we reviewed a few months later she was delighted to confide that her intimate life with her partner was much better because through the work we did she had become more empowered and finally was brave enough to share with her partner what she enjoys and what doesn't. A complete win-win situation.

You certainly have lived by experience and openly talk about the traumas you have encountered through your life; how do you stay so positive and upbeat?

By choosing the energy of gratitude. Having gratitude makes us more future-focused and keeps us in a positive mindset. The traumas I have experienced have all been life changing. Having experienced loss after loss I was truly brought to my knees both physically and spiritually.

I had nothing left, I had lost the people who meant the most to me, I had lost my physical freedom to paralysis, and I was an accidental addict through prescription drug addiction.

"At one point I even lost my sanity and if I allowed it, these traumas could have blighted the rest of my life, therefore, I made the decision to grow from my pain and to seek the beauty in my world."

The brain has a negative bias and if we don't take charge, we can find ourselves victims to our experiences and I never allowed myself to say, 'why me', it's not in my vocabulary.

 It never occurred to me to see myself as any different to anyone, I just kept believing in a better life that somewhere not far away that I had to somehow create.

Of course, I had to grieve, of course, I had to process what had happened, of course, I had to learn to walk and use my left hand again. I strongly believe that my emotional and physical recovery was born out of a love of life.

And also, by seeking out the beauty in my experiences and putting my hands together in gratitude for what I have learned and for who I have become.I am a better person for my painful experiences, I am grateful to have suffered.

Who inspires you and do you find yourself heartened by people's transformations through your practice?

My inspiration comes from so many areas, especially the natural world. I truly believe that nature holds so much wisdom.

We only have to look at the cycle of the seasons to be reminded that change is just around the corner and to hang on.

But if you want to know about people who inspire me, I love to absorb the wisdom of people like Maya Angelou, Eckart Tolle, Bruce Lipton, and Oprah Winfrey but really, it's the people I work with that inspire me.

I am inspired by anyone who wants to change their lives. I get so fired up with vital energy when I get a call to say I want to do things differently or I want to live a better life. This inspires me .

Can you share any words of wisdom that helped you in your successful career?

Yes, always keep your authenticity and integrity.

Choose to be yourself in everything you do because you will attract the right clients that way.

HOWARD HUGHES

Leadership Development, Executive Coach

Contact:

Website: www.howardmhughes.com

*"You are the ultimate authority of your own life.
You are the guru. Learn how to set yourself apart
from the herd."*

his is your description of what you can teach people, what sets you apart from the herd?

Great question. Could you not have picked an easier one to start with? I think the best way to illustrate the point is to tell the story of the cows and rhino:

Once upon a time there was a beautiful lush green pasture that held a herd of cows. They would roam the pasture grazing, ruminating, sleeping and repeat day after day. One day, one of the calves came up to his mother and asked - what's over there beyond that jungle?

The mother replied "Some say that it's a beautiful place - wide open spaces, lakes, mountains, different views but that's not for us"

The calf asked if anyone had ever gone there to which the mother replied that very, very few had but they never return. To the mother's surprise the calf said they would like to try. The mother was horrified!

"Why would you want to leave? You have all you can eat, the warmth and safety of the herd, very few predators... you have it all!" But as the calf got older there was a restlessness in her that outweighed her comfort and so she went to the head of the herd and expressed her desire to leave. "There'll be no coming back" said the head of the herd. "If you leave us you can never return, you'll be rejected the same way you are rejecting us now. Why do you want to go when you have everything here? Your family, your friends, food, security..." But the cow wanted to go.

Off the cow went towards the jungle. At the edge she saw rhinos charging through the undergrowth while other rhinos on the far side shouted instructions - "look out, a trap - look out, a hunter - look out, dense growth go around!"

She noticed that the rhinos giving instructions had scars from where they had been hurt. In her heart she had an image of what the promised land look like and it drew her to take the first step. She was nervous at first but she began to gather pace and she could hear what the other rhinos were saying to her.

She followed their instructions and eventually (having avoided some traps but being caught in others) getting out through her own resilience; she got up again and made it through the jungle to the promised land.

She walked slowly over to a beautiful lake to take a well-earned drink. When she bent down to drink, she caught her reflection in the water. She was not a cow but a rhino. And when she looked up she saw the landscape of unimaginable beauty and a vast expanse of freedom.

She turned to her fellow rhinos and said - "I'm not a cow..." to which one of the rhinos said "Look again at the herd you left..."

To her surprise, everyone on the other side of the jungle was a rhino but their deep-held and unquestioning beliefs had them convinced they were all cows and they behaved accordingly." The term 'herd' in this case is not a pejorative term. In biology, there is a term, homeostasis where there is an equilibrium between interdependent elements in an ecosystem.

People like to fit in - with family, neighborhoods, society and national identity. No-one is an island, but many sacrifice their individuality to maintain this equilibrium.

Through my own choices but also recognising that I didn't do it alone, I have made and lost a lot. It has been a great learning experience. I have been through the jungle to a greater extent than many but to a lesser extent than others. The net result is that I am now at a place where I can enjoy the view but also assist other rhinos that choose to make the journey. I have the scars!

Have you always had an interest in coaching or did someone/ something else lead you down this professional path?

For my brief stint in U.C.D., I took psychology as one of my subjects in my late teens and one of the first books that I didn't just read but consume in my early twenties was The Celestine Prophecy by James Redfield.

I've always had an interest in improving the current situation. I think I get that from my mum and her mum in turn. It's a drive towards the positive rather than a recoil from the negative.

Have you ever met people who you consider having great success but don't have the mindset to enjoy it? Isn't that a pity?

So, my interest is in enhancing the existing rather than fixing something that's broken. Although there is a bit of an overlap.

My career initially was in desktop publishing, running film and bromide for design houses and then in the production end of advertising and graphic design (I was a digital finished artist)

Looking to improve my own situation I decided to do something else that I loved - DJing. While I was working hard, I discovered that I had hit a ceiling. When I got married and became a dad, I knew this was an unsustainable lifestyle, so I turned my attention to what I had a passion for. It was actually a lifestyle business - direct sales in personal development - that allowed me to create my exit strategy. The work I did on myself began to show.

To enhance it I decided to get a formal qualification, so I took a higher diploma in Life & Executive Coaching. To add further value, I also went and trained as a fire walk Instructor.

Can you share what becoming a 'fire walk Instructor' entails and what kind of training it is?

Becoming a fire walk Instructor was an amazing experience. As I say to people, this is the action part to the theory of personal development.

When you consider some facts about fire and human skin-

- at 45° C - 51° C skin damage occurs in 1 minute
- at 52° C - 70° C skin damage occurs in seconds
- from 70° C upwards skin damage occurs in milliseconds and
- a car engine melts at 200° C
- the temperature of the coals is between 400° C - 500° C.

The nearest Fire walk Instructors to me were in Switzerland in order for me to get my qualification. I was there for a week in a quaint log cabin that was over a century old- I was told. There were only two students, and we were straight in that evening with a small 1m x 2m fire. When I look at it now, it was so small. Then, it looked like the gaping mouth of hell, and I questioned my mental state for being there.

For the week we had daily classes which incorporated arrow snapping (breaking arrows with the hollow of your throat), rebar bending (bending steal 9mm rebars used in construction with the hollow of your throat) and smashing blocks with your bare hands.

Each exercise designed to expand your mind from the confines of what you think is possible for yourself.

We also did glass walking (literally walking on broken glass in your bare feet) and we also washed each other's feet as an act of humility and also recognising that each of us is a temple that houses the Divine.

It culminated in a 40ft firewall which we had built ourselves. For some doubters of the fire walk experience who say that you are not on the coals to burn your feet - this was the tester.

For me, this wasn't the toughest of the Fire walks. On one of the days we built a small fire away from the cabin; maybe about 3 meters in length. As the coals glowed everyone else walked off to the cabin. Left alone with the fire they told me it was up to me whether I wanted to walk or not.

No was looking and no-one was judging. It was the most powerful, introspective experience.

Usually in fire walks you'd be in a crowd.

Even with the four of us there - two instructors and two students - it was enough to give a higher buzz. You could 'borrow' some energy, as it were. There, alone in the Alps with the fire is something I'll never forget.

"It's about not looking for reward in every action or interaction. I think office politics can be a big hindrance here, where some people are promoted on the credit of work that you have done or where people compromise standards in order to get the bonus"

How has the pandemic affected your business and how did you manage the initial isolation both professionally and personally?

Not much changed for me during the pandemic. My life was and is in the home. Marketing and training in the morning, Daddy Daycare in the afternoon and then back to interviewing my leads in the evening. This works best for me as I advertise in different time zones.

My wife, Mary took the home office and myself and the kids worked from the kitchen table. I can't emphasise enough the importance of having some sort of timetable to work to. Self-discipline is key. Self-mastery is also key when you are all living in the same space so closely and for such a long period of time.

Cabin fever can creep in under your conscious awareness but when you get slightly depressed and snappy it's time to go for a walk! It's time for a change of scenery.

The school were excellent at continuing to provide the curriculum online so there was a template there. Thankfully, the weather was also excellent so the kids could play in the front and back gardens. With technology being what it is nowadays, the kids could communicate with their friends online.

So as such, there was never a rock-bottom sense of isolation. Additionally, the Friday Virtual BON meetings where you and I met were great to bridge the temporary restrictions.

> *"I'm human and I do like rewards and recognition*
> *when they are spontaneous or as a random act.*
> *These are the perks of life that I think enhance it"*

Professionally, I think it has done more good for my business, as people started and are starting to develop a 'lifestyle'. People are no longer afraid of 'the void' that comes from when you have time to relax. Families reconnected with their kids and partners, got reacquainted - caught up. I think the pace of life has people always looking to be 'busy' and they feel a sense of guilt or waste if they're not doing something, if they are idle for any period of time.

"What could I be doing instead?" Again, if you have timetable, a visual representation of how you are spending your time it is actually more freeing than restrictive (talking from personal experience - it's a paradigm shift I had to make)

It is also recognition of how you spent your time which is as immensely beneficial as knowing where you are going to spend your time.

Can you share any words of wisdom that helped you in your successful career?

Do it because it's the right thing to do and do it with a grateful heart. To some, it may seem like a simple statement but it's really quite a challenge. Something it has taken me years if not decades to achieve. It's difficult because it means the shedding of our most basic survival instincts; to amass. It is the subjugation of the ego that is driven by gain or fear of loss

In the great book - Drive: The Hidden Determinants of Human Behaviour by Daniel Pink. I learned that rewards are addictive. Brian Knutson - Professor of Psychology and Neuroscience, National Institute of Alcohol Abuse and Alcoholism found that dopamine is released to the nucleus accumbens when people are offered a reward.

This is the same reaction as addiction and causes people to go from risk-averse to risk-seeking behaviour.

I find now a better or lasting reward than a job well done for the right reason. When you do it with a grateful heart then there is added energy, fun and the time flies. Controlling your inner reward means you'll never be disappointed and, paradoxically the more you receive in return.

As Garth Brooks said "You are never truly rich
until you have something money can't buy"

RUSS HEDGE

Inspirational Specialist,
Coach and Author

Contact:

Website:www.russhedge.com
Twitter: russhedge

*C*an you give the Talk Learn Connect (TLC) audience a summary of your professional path and what brought you from sales to coaching?

I have had quite a journey over the past year. This time a year ago I was Sales and Marketing Manager at Servpro of LInn and Benton Counties in Corvallis, Oregon. I had been there for approximately seven years. Previously, I had been in Sales and Marketing in a company in Salem Oregon for about seventeen years. All in all, I have thirty plus years of Sales and Marketing experience.

My favorite part of my job has always been Marketing and connecting with people. In my last job I was able to do a lot of speaking, coaching and training for my team and others that I connected with.

So, about a year ago

I began to look into starting my own business on the side - Russ Hedge Coaching and Consulting.

I had just begun to get all the foundation of my business together... and then Covid arrived.

This became the perfect time to pivot and go full steam ahead with my business and break out on my own.

I have never looked back. I am coaching, speaking, podcasting, and I have a new book coming out in mid-October- "Befuddled? Live the Life You Choose!" And I am definitely living the life I choose.

You say that successful networking "...is the life blood of your business and I can teach you how to Network and Connect driving great prospects to your business" - What kind of teaching methods do you implement in your business?

Successful networking comes from true connection. I have a fun and systematic approach to connection and by teaching you how to network and connect, I help you to build a community that is there to support your business. After all, connecting is really building true friendships... and friends want to help friends.

What I teach enables you to make true connections that are your Core Advocates! People who will advocate for you; core advocates want to truly help because they care about you and all you are doing.

The best way to begin this process is to care about them and show interest in all they are doing. Be authentic and be an advocate for them, because, as John Maxwell says "People don't care how much you know until they know how much you care.

Many businesses here in Ireland have been innovative in the way they will now have to operate, post-pandemic. How has the pandemic affected your business, and have you had to pivot your business online?

Since my business began with a giant pivot, I have done nothing but benefit from the pandemic. The push online gave me a great platform to build my business quickly and connect with people all over the world.

Creativity and innovation have been the path to my early success. I have also taken action and moved forward, figuring out things as I go. I believe you find your purpose (or Why) and then move forward and make it happen. We all need to learn and grow with our business and realize change is inevitable.

As I slowly reintegrate with people in person, I have learned that online platforms have now become a necessary and permanent part of my business.

The word 'Community' throughout lockdown and the pandemic, has been applied so many times on social media, in articles and on news platforms. How essential is this word to you and what you practice?

Community is what true connection is all about. Through genuine networking, I have been able to build my community worldwide. This community has already helped me in many areas of my business as I work to support others and help them in theirs!

Community is essential to any business's success. It always has been, and it is even more important today in our current climate

I love people and making new friends is my passion, so it has been a true joy to take my local community and expand it all over the world.

Can you share any words of wisdom that helped you in your successful career?

I have several words of wisdom from mentors that have shaped me and how I do business, but here are two of them:

> *"Don't wait to start until you know everything...*
> *just get going, Learn, Adapt, and Grow"*

It is important to get started and take action a 'Do It Now Attitude' gets things done.

My journalism professor in college used to tell me, "Just do the next dumb thing!" This means to get unstuck whether it is in writing, or life, just move forward and do something.

Forward motion builds momentum. I talk about these words of wisdom further in my new book, "Befuddled? Live the Life You Choose!"

PAMELA FINN

PR Director, TV Presenter, Media Agency Director

Contact:

Website: www.prpam.ie

Instagram: Pamela Finn

*Y*our background includes a variety of mediums – Journalism, Radio, TV Presenting and Public Relations. Media is where you are drawn to, have you always had an interest in this type of profession?

Ever since I can remember I have wanted to work in media, in particular - TV. Growing up in a family of seven children meant I always had someone to play with, and we created our own theatre shows, and then acted them out in front of the 'audience', this is where the love and passion developed - to entertain and tell a good story, your average sibling can be a tough critic after all!!

I remember clearly - being offered a sales job in Galway, when I was about 19, the money was incredible. At the same time, Independent Radio in Dublin offered me a role, the salary was almost half, but it meant a foot in the door to media. I never looked back, and I continue today to just keep following that dream. The role in radio was in sales and sponsorship, I was always afraid to take that leap into the presenting world, I didn't think I had what it took.

I would spend my evenings in East Coast Radio and any place that would allow me in the door to see how they worked; I was like a sponge. I wanted to know it all, yet I had no qualification, just a gut instinct I could do it. A couple of years later I went back to college to study journalism, worked in a local newspaper and set up a PR agency - anything to work in media!

A few years ago, after a chance encounter with a Hollywood coach, I decided to just go for it and do a presenting course with him and hone my skills. That coach recommended me for an audition. Fast forward six years, and I had my own show on Sky 191 Irish TV, as well as working on the RTE show At Your Service as their PR expert.

Most recently my sister company Hashtag Media launched 'Social TV' which is TV for social media platforms.

I love storytelling, and believe everyone has a story, it's great to meet someone for an interview and find out what makes them tick, sometimes a simple conversation can take you to another place entirely.

Can you explain in more detail what your marketing initiative 'Social TV' can offer for events?

Social TV was forged as a meeting of social media and television style broadcasting, it offers snippets of interviews at events, everything from attendees to speakers right through to a virtual walk through of the event - it has proven to increase attendances at these events.

The passive viewer (someone that is watching TV, working and looking at their phone screen) is a huge audience for social media; we capture that in a few minutes. People do not have the attention span to watch a 30-minute show - they want to know what you have and do they want it in about one minute!

Can you recall any events that didn't go to plan, and did you learn any lessons from it?

No event goes to plan, if it did, we would not be pushing ourselves enough and getting complacent, there is always room for improvement. At one event the videographer didn't tell us the sound that was recorded could not be used as it was barely audible-they didn't bring the right equipment. This taught me a hard lesson - ALWAYS hire someone that is better than you, double-check everything and ask questions.

From chatting to guests here on TLC, there is a mixed reaction how the pandemic has affected their business. How has the pandemic affected your business?

I spoke with media mogul Norah Casey last week about this, a pandemic is an opportunity to grow to adapt. 80 per cent of the most successful companies in the world were forged in a recession. This is time for huge change.

I'm mainly mentoring businesspeople now in PR and offering strategies to make sure they have a vision. So many businesses have had to change their business model.

In terms of Social TV - this is about to explode, there has been a 67 per cent increase in people buying online, that is incredible - if they are online browsing - they are viewing. We just received news that we are media partners for World Skills Ireland - creating video content for them to share on their platforms.

We are keeping busy creating mini social series for social media, it's the ideal time to rethink and recalibrate.

Can you share any words of wisdom that helped you in your successful career?

The mentor also needs a mentor. I am always asking questions, looking for advice.I reach out to people that are successful in their perspective fields - and ask how can I do better?

What can I do differently?

IRIAL O'FARRELL

Coach, Trainer, Consultant and Author

Contact:

Website: www.evolutionconsulting.ie

*C*an you share with the TLC audience, what you offer to your customers and what your business- Evolution Consulting's approach is?

Evolution Consulting is a bespoke coaching, training and consulting company, with the key purpose of maximising clients' effective business performance.

As principal consultant, I take a look at what is going on with the company through five lenses -

Strategy: Is there a clear vision, purpose and fit-for-purpose strategy that is guiding the business?

If so, has it been clearly cascaded down through each of the functions? In my experience, strategies tend to be framed in terms of a 'Strategic To-Do' list, rather than understanding what game the company is playing.

Structure: Is the infrastructure of the company working for it or has it been outgrown? The infrastructure of many organisations tends to evolve over time, in response to needs rather than due to deliberate intention.

Sometimes, lower business performance is an unintended consequence. Infrastructure deals with both organisational design and organisational processes such as performance management and recruitment etc.

Culture: Is the culture conducive to what the business is seeking to achieve? Asking people to suddenly become "innovative" when they've spent the last ten years adhering to regulations is just not going to happen, no matter how often or politely they're asked.

Capability: Do the right people have the right competencies to enable the business to succeed?

Change: Is there really a desire to put in the hard work necessary to achieve the desired outcome? Change initiatives being led by leaders who say they want change in a 'now go off over there and sort that out' kind-of way, will firmly fall into the seventy-four per cent of transformation projects that fail.

What Evolution Consulting offers clients is -

- A diagnosis as to what issues are negatively impacting organisational, team and individual performances
- A thoughtful, comprehensive design and plan as to how they can change the dynamics
- Services such as Strategy and Organisation Design workshops, Leadership and Management Development programmes, Executive Coaching, to support and develop planning, design and implementation capability
- Change management guidance and support during the scary rollercoaster of implementation.

Where did your instinctive passion for organisational dynamics and boosting businesses, performance come from?

It's going to sound extremely geeky when I say this, but the first inkling of my passion came in my first job, in Sydney Australia.

I was fascinated with why everyone loved one manager and disliked ('hate' is possibly a bit too strong) another. While fascinated by it, I didn't pay it too much thought, as I forged a career in Fund Administration. I quickly moved into management and developed a high performing team. It wasn't called a high performing team in those days, I'm not sure the term had been coined by then.

"However, you know a team is high performing when, due to my appointment to an internal organisation design project, other managers were outbidding each other to get their hands on the team members"

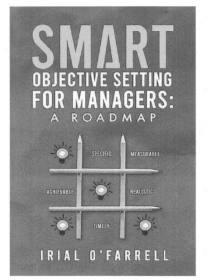

As it came pretty naturally to me, I assumed management came naturally to others too. As I've learned over the last twenty years, for many, they were promoted into management, based on their strong technical ability, not their ability to manage. And no, it doesn't come naturally to them, they sometimes need a bit of a helping hand.

For me, it was always about matching the ability of the individual to the performance needs of the business. Different work is designed to happen at different levels and functions within an organisation. It is designed, both in terms of the role/level/function and in terms of the price the product or service is set at.

If a task is designed and priced to be done at one level and is done (or done again) at a more senior level, that task has become very costly.

Not just in terms of the cost of the time for the more senior person to do the task but also in terms of the opportunity loss of the task (and it's impact) that the more senior person should have been spending their time doing.

Don't ask me where that bit came from. I studied science in college, not finance!

You became an accredited Change Master, with the Change Management Institute, earlier this year. Can you explain this further?

Yes, I'd be delighted to. This is the number one accreditation that I am truly proud of because it is like the apex of a mountain of boulders, made up of many, many different elements. Firstly, let me explain what an Accredited Master of Change means. The Change Management Institute (CMI) have three levels – Foundation, Specialist and Master. Specialist indicates a demonstrated ability to effect change within a project while Master indicates a demonstrated ability to effect change across the organisation.

Would you believe, I started the process in 2018. Becoming a specialist involves demonstrating you have the competencies required to be a change manager.

In addition to the requirements, is five days of continuous development in related topics, submitting a 2,000-word essay on a specific change project and getting two referees to complete evaluation forms. All of that is then topped off with an interview. My interview was scheduled for Friday, 13th March, 2020.

Yes, that is the day after Leo made his announcement that the schools were closed, effective immediately. The three children were banished from the room for the duration.

Having successfully earned the Specialist title, I got my date for the Master evaluation. It consisted of an intense four hours, where I had to evaluate a change case study and then prepare two presentations - a twenty-minute presentation to the executive team and a five-minute presentation to a team impacted by the change; followed by another interview. The husband did a full evacuation for that one!

I was on an absolute high when I got the news that I had been accredited. I didn't think I could beat that feeling but when I got the formal email, saying that my name had been entered onto CMI's list of Accredited Masters, I clicked through to see that the only name entered under Ireland was mine.

I literally was walking on air.

You might be wondering why this accreditation meant so much to me. Effecting change pulls from so many different disciplines – strategy and vision, strategic thinking, planning, leadership, engaging communication, understanding and reading people, their actions and their words, coaching, training, analysis, influencing, emotional intelligence, trust, deep listening, curiosity...the list is endless.

To me, this accreditation was the apex of being able to pull all those strands together and be recognised for it. Not everyone can be an effective change manager. It is as much, if not more so, about the people as it is about the process.

In our current climate, how has your business managed, or have you had to modify your own strategies, comparable to what you provide to your clients?

Well, thanks to the very generous support of the Irish government, I've been able to take advantage of the trading-on-line voucher and pivot my business.

By incorporating an online teaching platform into my website, I have been able to move training courses online and extend my reach beyond just Ireland. I'm very excited to design and promote management and leadership development programmes that will make a difference.

One course that I'm particularly looking forward to getting out there is on Developing Others' Problem-Solving Skills. Managers tend to excel at solving problems but aren't so good at developing other people's problem-solving skills. Over time, this causes a huge bottleneck, as everyone is waiting for the manager to sort issues out. This course actually provides mana-gers with the mindset, skills and process needed to free up their own time while also motivating their employees.

The other thing that the trading voucher allowed me to do was to install an e-commerce platform. This opened up the opportunity to sell products and not just services.

Having already written a book – Values: Not Just for the Office Wall Plaque-How Personal and Company Values Intersect - the e-commerce platform and covid prompted me to get back to writing and this book squarely focused on performance.

It's called SMART Objective Setting for Managers and it provides a multi-dimensional understanding of SMART, performance objectives, the human and what can, and does, typically go wrong with objective setting.

Since I'm always a practical 'right, what do we need to do, to sort it out' kinda gal, it also gives managers a comprehensive understanding of what to do. While also making sure that objective setting and performance development works for the individual, the manager, the team and the business.

So long term, I feel Covid gave me an opportunity to pivot my business into an on-going sustainable business and freeing myself up more to work directly on the really juicy projects.

Can you share any words of wisdom that helped you in your successful career?

The best bit of advice I ever got was as part of feedback on a job interview. In the months prior to me setting up Evolution Consulting, the company I was working for indicated to me that it wasn't going to create a senior manager role for me in Learning and Development, the area I was working in. So, I interviewed for a senior manager role in an operational area I had an interest in. Unsuccessful, I arranged a feedback session.

The Vice President started off with the usual surfacy-type feedback and I just kept thinking "that's not it" so I kept pushing for what was the real reason I didn't get the promotion. This went on for four or five rounds until he had clearly run out of the easier stuff and knew he needed to give me something meaty.

And then it came - two key pieces of insight that have never left me: I didn't network enough. I didn't say "I want this job."

When I heard it, I knew these really were the reasons I didn't get the job. Now when I'm in potential talks with a client, I make sure that every single time, I work in an actual statement that I'd love to work with them. As for networking, this was the timeliest piece of advice I ever got.

By this stage, I was about to set up Evolution Consulting, facing into the reality of needing to network to generate business.

As I was in the process of completing my Executive Coaching qualification, I took the topic straight to my own coach and got to the bottom of what held me back from networking. Let me tell you, if you saw me at a networking event today, you would never, ever think I used to have an issue with it!

JEREMY MURPHY

Principal at JM Agency, Publishing Consultancy

Contact:

Website: www.jm.agency
Twitter: JeremyEditor

*Y*ou have a broad range of work experience from working as a contributor in the Irish Catholic to the Sunday Tribune, was this diversity of workplaces a deliberate choice or something else entirely?

A little bit of both really. I graduated in 2007, after which I worked in advertising sales. I stayed in that industry for two years, before going back into education.

After I finished my master's, I did freelance work as a journalist, and I also taught part-time in various colleges and schools. It was a choice in the respect I was yet to fully settle on a career.

I felt my mind and interests pulling me in contrasting directions, and I had yet to find a career I felt was the right fit for me.

However, the economic climate at the time certainly contributed to this; when I finished my masters in 09 the country was deep in recession.

It was hard to find permanent work and one couldn't be too choosy; I even took an unpaid internship at a local authority.

> *"JM Agency is a new venture, but I have been working as a book editor for a lot longer and I probably have a little more to impart in that field"*

Could you tell us about your campaign #atimetowrite?

Yes, I started that campaign as I felt the Covid19 pandemic was a perfect opportunity for people who may have considered writing in the past but never found the time to write.

These times we are living through are difficult in so many respects, but I do feel writing and works of the imagination can be cathartic. People often say times such as these exacerbate the need to create and people subsequently seek imaginative vents.

The #atimetowrite campaign consists of a series of social media posts, mostly creative writing exercises, poetry recitals and other content, aimed at stimulating and inspiring people. I also offer some free editing advice and tips.

What was it that brought you to where you are now, Principal at JM Agency, Publishing Consultancy, can you tell us something extra about what you offer that nobody else does?

While we are a comprehensive service, offering design and other publishing services, we have a distinctive philosophy of book editing, which continues to underline everything we do.

Having your book appraised by a professional editor can be daunting for writers, so a constructively critical, positive philosophy of editing is essential. It doesn't mean I am a soft editor; far from it.

It means if I think the writer is making a mistake, I will be honest and explain and analyse in detail, but I will also explain in detail what s/he is doing right. It usually means I have to take a bit longer appraising, and my Reports - and a sample of one can be viewed on my website - are very robust, but I feel the writer receives a better service in the end.

I was inspired by the great American writer John Updike, who remarked that a critic's role was to 'identify what the author is trying to achieve, and assess how close they come to it.' Our job as editors is not to tell our writers what to write, it is to help them achieve their own personal vision and write the best book they can. Our role is more akin to that of coach or inspiring mentor than ruthless critic. I was also inspired by the coaching philosophy of Sir John Whitmore, which I discovered when reading for a business diploma at Technological University Dublin.

I have read many articles on the effects of the pandemic for publishers and authors in relation to launching new books, which has not been good for both. But authors and publishers have found innovative ways to engage with their readers. What have you found that has helped you in an innovative way?

I think it is too early to assess the wider societal and economic impact of the pandemic. We don't know yet what changes will be long-term.

If there is a greater migration online, that will of course change everything. Not many people know this, but over 50% of books (certainly in the US) are already sold online, and if this figure increases dramatically, it will force retailers and publishers to adapt; they will have to adapt, or they will die. It has been suggested that publishers may sell more books directly through their website.

This is not necessarily a positive development for me, as this could have a negative impact on competition, but I would certainly agree that the current situation, where one e-commerce giant has a virtual monopoly on the online market, is not good either.

On a personal level, I think people are interacting and engaging more in social media and networking platforms. This is positive. I also feel people are forming more online communities as a result of the pandemic; rather than just interacting one on one, I have noticed a trend towards social media communities, and I would be very interested to see whether this is backed up by data.

If used properly, this can give smaller businesses like mine possibilities to grow their networks.

Can you share any words of wisdom that helped you in your successful career?

You have to think of your client; what are s/he's needs? What does s/he stand to gain by availing of your service?

This advice sounds simple, but it is very important when it comes to promoting your business and service.

PATRICK OSBORNE

Author, Playwright and Horticulturist

Contact:

Twitter: PaddyOsborne71
Facebook: Paddy Osborne

*C*an you give a summary of your career to date as it is quite a varied one?

My first job was selling newspapers when I was eleven. Today, it probably sounds like something from a Dicken's novel. The money was small, but the tips were great, especially selling papers in the pubs to fellas who were half cut. It's been all downhill ever since!

My grandparents had a coal yard and I used to help my granny with the scales and on the till.

There was a lot of poverty back then, especially in Dublin's inner city. Some people couldn't afford a full bag of coal so they would buy maybe a stone at a time. My granny was a lovely, kind woman and she always gave that extra little bit to people who were struggling.

As my interest in horticulture developed, I got a job in a gardening shop, Mackey's Seeds on Mary Street when I was still at school. The shop is long gone and is now the entrance to the Jervis Shopping centre.

After starting college in the National Botanic Gardens, Glasnevin, I got to work in many different parks all over Dublin. These included Merrion Square, the Royal Hospital Kilmainham and Malahide Castle. I also worked in Glasnevin Cemetery on the old side, where the Daniel O'Connell tower is situated. This was a fascinating place, steeped in history and well worth visiting.

"I was employed as a Fás supervisor, spending five years in an old Guinness estate on a fifty-acre site in Chapelizod, near Farmleigh. It was a stunning place and I loved it there"

After that I helped to set up a landscape and maintenance company called Cleansweep for the Daughters of Charity. The workers were adults with mild intellectual disabilities, and it was a very rewarding place to work. I spent another five years in this job and one of our main contracts was in Aras an Uachtaráin while President McAleese was in office. It was a brilliant experience.

In 2003, my wife Liz and I relocated to Kerry with our three young children - Robert, Rebecca and David. I spent the next nine years working as grounds manager for a large hotel group and again really enjoyed the challenge. I also set up my own landscape business and ran it successfully for over seven years but decided to get out of it at the end of the Celtic Tiger. I would have had to expand the business and get more involved in the construction end of things to survive.

This would have meant working anything from sixty to eighty hours a week, so I re-evaluated my situation and came to the conclusion that my family were more important. I have since taken up a gardening position with Kerry County Council which gives me a far better family, work and lifestyle balance.

'Killarney's answer to Roddy Doyle' as headlined in a local paper, that is some comparison, how does it make you feel?

I was mortified but delighted at the same time as I'm a massive fan of Roddy's. I read The Commitments while at college, I was about nineteen at the time and it was just before the film was made. I was totally hooked.

I've since read most of Roddy's books; I loved Paddy Clarke Ha Ha Ha as it could have easily been my own childhood. I also loved his television series The Family based around his novel The Woman Who Walked into Doors.

How have you managed during the lockdown/pandemic on a personal and professional level?

I'm one of the lucky ones, in that my job with the Council was classed as an essential service so apart from the initial three weeks of lockdown I've been working away full-time.

My wife, Liz is a nurse so again she has been constantly in work.

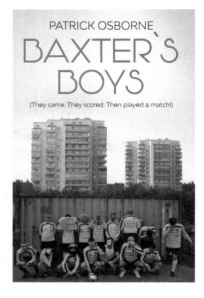

PATRICK OSBORNE

BAXTER'S BOYS

(They came. They scored. Then played a match!)

I'm also a referee with the FAI and an underage coach with my local GAA club, Killarney Legion.

My sons, Robert and David were away in college so they can back home fulltime also my daughter, Rebecca's job shut down, so she was also at home full-time.

We all had to get used to living with each other once again only this time there were five adults living under the one roof.

One the hardest things for me personally were not being able to visit my family and friends in Dublin, especially my parents, my dad is eighty-one and my Mam is seventy-nine this year. The other thing I really missed was sport.

As writers, we are comfortable with isolation life, have you begun another book or have an idea for another?

I'm comfortable in my own company so I can quite easily get lost in a book. I did find writing difficult to concentrate on initially even though I had a number of projects and ideas to work on.

Prior to lockdown myself and some friends had set up a drama group called the Four Esquires and we had successfully staged several short plays. We had to shelve our plans to put on other plays. I did get to develop two more and all going well we will put them on soon.

The lockdown presented a new challenge in marketing my debut novel, Baxter's Boys, so that has been a very worthwhile experience. I've also been working on my second novel. It's a dark comedy, a kidnapping caper set in Dublin.

I don't want to give too much away about it at the moment but as part of the research I spent an afternoon in Mountjoy prison where I almost started a riot.

Can you share any words of wisdom that helped you in your successful career?

I'm not sure if I can pass on words of wisdom but I've picked up a few bits and pieces along the way which have definitely helped me. The number one rule I try to live by is to be an active participant in your own rescue.

No matter what you do in life or what you hope for you need to ask yourself what am I doing about it and is it enough?

A coach once told me that you have two ears and only one mouth so try to listen twice as much as you talk.

After all, you already know what you're going to say but if you listen you might learn something new. I definitely try to be courteous and respectful to everyone whether you're the tea lady or the CEO of a multinational company.

If you don't treat people fairly well then, I've no interest in you as you've lost my respect.

WENDY SLATTERY

Co-Founder and CEO of Beauty Buddy

Contact:

Website: www.thebeautybuddy.com

*C*an you give us a summary of your company and what inspired you to develop this type of business?

Beauty Buddy is a data analytics company dedicated to the beauty and cosmetic industry. Ultimately its aim is to bridge the gap between brands and consumers in an €800bn industry.

Beauty Buddy, the app, is an inclusive community of Beauty Buddies made up of real, honest, independent and trusted peer to peer users. They connect with each other to learn about and decide which beauty, skincare and wellness products to buy.

Harnessing the power of this unique, trusted and independent beauty community, the app takes into account everything it knows about the user and recommends the best products, reviews, ratings, tutorials etc. relevant to that user. My sister, co-founder and COO of Beauty Buddy, Tracy Leavy and I always had that 'want' to create a global business/brand that provided an everyday solution to a problem.

"The app can extract real-time insights, analytics and actionable data that is invaluable to brands and industry partners. This also includes access to consumer behaviours, competitive comparisons and sentiment analysis"

It wasn't until we came across that 'problem' whilst being over-whelmed when shopping for a make-up brush one day that we believed there was an opportunity to create a solution that currently did not exist on the market.

We began to talk and research the market and ultimately discovered that the data we were set to capture gave us a competitive advantage. This data enabled us to fill a void as a dedicated beauty analytics company.

Throughout this pandemic must have been a busy time for you as potential 'new customers' where isolating at home. This pandemic must have been somewhat a 'positive' for your business?

As a start-up, we are constantly busy. We are a team of 11 who, like many others, found ourselves working from home, with added family commitments. However, with the right team and culture in place, lock down showed us how small the world is when it comes to opportunity.

That was a positive for the business.

Whilst the world isolated at home, this brought with it increased online traffic to social media, online news and other platforms that offered a distraction.

As we saw an increase in usage and trends, we were able to use our creativity to drive new marketing and user sampling campaigns, retail and brand on boarding initiatives etc. alongside hitting business milestones and pitching to investors.

Following on from previous question, how have you coped during the pandemic, both on a personal level and a professional one?

Really well thank you, I am incredibly lucky that my family is safe, well and keeping busy. Lockdown afforded us all the opportunity to take some time to appreciate how short life is which in turn only fueled our personal and professional ambitions.

We are privileged that our continued dedication to the vision of Beauty Buddy and the support of our team has enabled our start-up to thrive in unexpected circumstances.

We have big plans for the business, and we are excited to bring these to market both in Ireland and globally.

Did you find beauty 'Influencers' to show case your product and explain it more or did it happen completely organically? Sometimes its all about good timing?

Beauty Buddy has received a hugely positive response from brands, retailers, and the public. The word 'Influencers' has different meanings to different people. We have engaged with several social media influencers as part of our marketing strategy. Our audience has grown organically alongside this thanks to the functionality of the app and the ever-growing community of beauty buddies who recommend the app to friends, family and social media followers etc.

We look to 'Influencers' within the brand and retail industry who work with us to develop the data analytics.

This in turn will bring immense benefits to the sector by changing how brands will inevitably create and market their products to customers.

"We have big plans for the business, and we are excited to bring these to market both in Ireland and globally"

Can you share any words of wisdom that helped you in your successful career?

I believe experiences in life and previous business lessons have enabled us to gain the wisdom we needed to guide us through our start-up journey. We learn by 'doing', taking chances and not being afraid to fail.

We encourage our team to be creative and to explore new ways of doing things.

We then have processes in place to critique our actions which allows us to be innovative and achieve our goals.

MICHELLE MAHER

Regional Development Officer for See Her Elected (SHE)

Contact:

Website: www.seeherelected.ie
Twitter: Michelle Maher

*C*an you share your background and what area of profession you are in currently?

At school I always loved science and after getting a place in National University of Ireland (NUI) Galway to study zoology, I thought that I was sorted for life! Little did I know. A letter from the civil service offering me a job knocked me off course and I packed my bags and headed to Dublin - lured by the thought of a wage and living in the Big Smoke.

I can't remember the grade, but it was one of the lower ones, at the time and you got a pay rise annually regardless of how much or how little work you did. I was grumbling about the inequity of this to a flat mate who worked for an international pension's consultancy.

She told me that there was a vacancy in the administration department and that I should apply. I did, and that led to a fifteen-year career in the pensions industry and by progressing and passing all the industry-relevant exams, I ended up as a Consultant in the Employee Benefits Division.

After a few years out of the workforce to meet family commitments, I took yet another career swerve and went to Maynooth University as a now, mature and much more sensible student. A degree in politics and history was followed by a PhD and lecturing on the University's politics degree. 2020 saw me leaving academia and joining See Her Elected (SHE).

"If you have ever been told 'sure that's the way it's always been', or 'This is the way things are done around here' - then you have found an informal institution!"

When and why was See Her Elected (SHE) developed?

SHE was established in 2019 as a partnership programme between Longford Women's Link and 50:50 Northwest. We are funded by the Department of Housing, Local Government and Heritage. SHE's purpose is to support women into political life, with a particular emphasis on the rural constituencies of the Northwest and Midlands. Some, predominantly urban councils are there or thereabouts when it comes to equal representation for men and women, for example, Dublin City and Dun Laoghaire - Rathdown.

Others, for example, Meath and Kildare are at 60:40 in favour of men. But it is a very different story in rural counties. Donegal has thirty-seven county councilors, only four of them are women. Sligo, Roscommon and Leitrim each have eighteen councilors with only three women in each. Longford only elected a single woman councilor, with a second being appointed to replace a male councilor who was successful in his bid to become a TD in February 2020.

So, it is obvious that there is something specific happening that is leaving women in rural Ireland severely under-represented in political institutions.

Although SHE was established to support women in the rural constituencies of the Northwest and Midlands region, moving online to circumnavigate Covid-19 restrictions means women outside of our intended region have an opportunity to benefit from our work.

In your opinion, why is there such an imbalance in gender ratio, in not only the political arena but across the board in many professional areas?

It's a combination of factors but if I had to pick one, it would be the informal institutional structures of society. Examples of informal institutions are conventions and patterns of behaviour.

"If you have ever been told 'sure that's the way it's always been', or 'this is the way things are done around here', then you have found an informal institution! "Informal institutions stick over time and become accepted by many as the normal way of doing things.

To see one example of this playing out in practice - a typical GAA club is a good place to look. Being part of a GAA club is acknowledged in political research as a key network to have at your disposal if you have political ambition. But men and women usually have very different roles in a club. Men are coaching the teams, holding key committee positions and other areas that are central to the success of the club.

Women are to be found transporting junior players, fundraising, maybe acting as secretary. And that's the way it has always been – the normal way the functions in a club are divided up. But one set of activities can be converted much more easily into tangible political capital when required, and it's not the network of sandwich makers!

Are there many people that inspire you and what is it that you find encouraging and motivating about them?

Oh, that's a good question!

There is a member of my family dealing with a particular set of circumstances with dignity and courage that makes me immensely proud, and I know their actions have been inspirational to many others, myself included. In terms of public figures, I am drawn to those who exhibit both integrity and intelligence and who have done interesting things with their lives.

So, among those I admire are Mary Robinson especially since she started podcasting and I discovered her sense of humor!

I have just finished reading Rosita Boland's book Elsewhere and I admire how determined and fearless a traveler she is. She would give anyone courage to take a step into the unknown. Rosita talks too about life rarely turning out the way you thought; but it is what you have and too short to waste. It's no harm being reminded of that.

Can you share any words of wisdom that helped you in your successful career?

I was part of a charity cycle and when faced with a tough climb at the end of a long day I was ready to give up. But a more experienced cyclist kept pace with me and got me to repeat the mantra 'I can, I will', with every slow rotation of the pedals.

It worked. I got there.

I still find myself repeating those words to myself when the going gets tough, often without immediately realising what I am doing.

And they still work.

CATHERINE THOMPSON

Fashion Influencer, Stylist

Contact:

Instagram: Catherine's Closet
Facebook: Catherine's Closet

*C*an you share a summary of your career to date and what led you down the path of fashion?

My daughter asked my mother what I was like as a child. Her reply was' she loved her style from a very early age.' Being the youngest of six children, I got a lot of hand-me-down clothes so as soon as I got a part-time job, I spent all my money on clothes.

I would spend hours looking in clothes shops and trying on clothes. I only wore an outfit once, so I decided to start selling my clothes online. It took off so well, I then started to order more styles and sizes of what I loved, and my business took off from there.

> *"I've done a business course, but it's really*
> *the personal end of meeting people and styling*
> *them that I'm passionate about most."*

Who is your biggest icon/s and inspiration for your style?

From a young age, it was Madonna, I loved how unique she was, always changing her image and still doing what she does best. The next icon for me was Princess Diana, in particular when she made her entrance in 'that' wedding dress.

My more recent icon is Tara Maynard. To me, she is a style queen. Millie MacIntosh is another person whom I love to follow. Her style is so effortless and chic.These people, for me, have the most influence on my style and vision.

How has the pandemic affected your business, and have you had to adjust it more to online or was it that way pre-pandemic?

A lot of my business is based in the home as I invite clients to be styled there so there was a huge negative effect for me.

That all had to cease for the last three months and more.I also buy my clothing pieces for my clients overseas so that all stopped as well.

There weren't any online orders either as people were going nowhere.

Do you, as a 'fashion influencer' integrate social media as a necessary business tool for you to grow your business?

One hundred percent social media is my business tool. Word of mouth is still a powerful old-fashioned mechanism for new business clients. When I style a client and they receive compliments, this is all good praise for me and what I do.

Can you share any words of wisdom that you received that helped you in your successful career?

If you are really passionate about what you do, stick with it.

There are so many ups and downs when starting your own business and trying to make it work. It's the best feeling in the world styling someone and making them feel good.

But if you really love what you do, it will be enough to make you so happy.

LORRAINE KEANE

Broadcaster, Journalist, TV Presenter

Contact:

Instagram: Lorraine Keane
Facebook: Lorraine Keane

*Y*ou studied Broadcasting and Journalism at Ballyfermot College **and you were drawn more to the broadcasting/presenting side. Did you enjoy the writing side of Journalism, and have you written anything or are you writing now?**

I have always liked performing. I was the first to put my hand up in school in singing class and I always wanted to study drama.

Unfortunately, being a child of 7 there were no after school activities, so I had to make do with improvisations at home with my very large family as my audience (laughs).

I tried to get into Trinity College Dublin Drama Degree but with absolutely no formal training or experience only made it to the last 100.

I also love writing and devour news daily. It was my best friend Ali- we are friends since we were 4 years old - found the broadcasting & journalism course for me.

It seemed to play to my passions and strengths so I thought I would give it a go. I absolutely loved it especially presenting on camera, from there I auditioned for AA Road watch, and it all went on from there.

What beauty treatment/essential have you missed the most in isolation?

My hairdressers Dylan Bradshaw definitely. Apart from it being a necessity, the team are like a little extended family to me.

I miss the company of all these talented young people and the pampering too.

You have a deep connection to charities like Trocaire and World Vision and have visited the countries that benefit from these charities. How do you feel when you return from these poverty-stricken countries?

I have done ten trips in ten years across the developing world. They are very difficult trips to do and they don't get any easier but I always try to look for the positive in everything.

Knowing I am helping to improve their lives gets me through it especially in the weeks when I come back.

I focus on getting as much publicity for the charity to increase awareness of the families I met who are struggling to survive. I have access to media and to the public - it is very important to me to use my profile to share these stories, which helps to raise funds and save lives.

Fashion Relief like most events was cancelled this year because of Covid -19, do you feel life will be different now in the future for such events like this?

I am using the time to get my fundraising initiative for Oxfam, Fashion Relief, online. This will turn Fashion Relief into a global fundraiser which potentially will make it even bigger - every cloud....

The families I met in the largest refugee camp in the world last December need us now more than ever... and when people are not earning obviously charities suffer the most.

It is not their fault they live where they live, they were just born in a place that has an extreme climate and as a result more natural disasters per annum. They cannot leave, they cannot afford to and even if they could, risking their lives, the world has shown how they are not wanted in most countries. It is very sad.

We are the lucky ones. We owe it to them. We have to help those living in extreme poverty. We have so much, and they have so little- some nothing at all.

I don't think we should have a choice.

"We in the developed world have caused the most damage to our planet yet it is those living in the world's poorest countries who are suffering the most"

Can you share any words of wisdom that helped you in your successful career?

I always tell my girls 'A smile and good manners will get you through life I've added - 'and education is important too' in more recent times now they are teenagers.

Be kind and considerate to others, treat others how you would like to be treated. And count your blessings.

I count my blessings every day for my healthy babies and wonderful family. It's all that matters in the end.

MONA LYDON-ROCHELLE

Poet, Author and Professor in Epidemiology

Contact:

Website: www.monalydon.com

*C*ould you give a summary of your career to date and what you are passionate about in your profession?

I hold a BS from the University of New Mexico, MS from Case Western Reserve University, and MPH and PhD from the University of Washington. My academic career spanned nearly 30 years, in which I researched maternal and child health, with a specific focus on the prevention and outcomes of Caesarean Section. During those years I served as a consultant to the World Health Organization (WHO),

National Institute of Health, and the Center for Disease Control and Prevention on both national and international research projects.

However, my mission with Médecins Sans Frontières (MSF), investigating the epidemic of multi-drug resistant tuberculosis in Abkhazian and Georgia was the most rewarding by far.

Notably, I finished my epidemiology tenure at the National Perinatal Epidemiology Centre in Cork, which I loved. I am passionate about motherhood and assuring the health of newborns.

Do you have another connection to Ireland other than as a professor in epidemiology and high-risk obstetrics at University College Cork?

I grew up in the small coastal town of Scituate, Massachusetts—coined the Irish Riviera because almost everyone was an Irish émigré or first-generation offspring. As children we were steeped in Irish songs, fairy tales, food and superstitions. We still have family in Cork and while at UCC, they were a tremendous support. It is more than sentimentality, I am proud of my Irish ancestry, family name and the remarkable poetic and Christian traditions. Notably, when missioned by Médecins Sans Frontières (MSF) out of the New York City office, MSF requested that I obtain Irish Citizenship (which I did) because placement of Irish Citizens in volatile countries was more straightforward than placing Americans!

You are also a poet. This seems like a diverse career change, or did it feel like a more natural path to progress to? Tell us what you like to write about in your poems.

Transitioning from epidemiology to poetry was somewhat seamless—the rigors of research, the discipline of scientific writing (publish or perish) and the ability to accept rejection—all are required in being a good poet. I owe a special debt to Paul Fitterer SJ, a Pacific Northwest Jesuit, who encouraged me to write poetry despite the seeming insanity of giving up tenure and a great salary!

Also, I believe I was born with a natural inclination toward the poetic-my father, James Kelleher Lydon, who passed when I was only one year old was a solicitor and poet. I read his tattered poems repeatedly.

> *"Because of Covid, performances and readings*
> *have all been cancelled but interviews such*
> *as yours and Jeremy Murphy's have promoted*
> *book sales thankfully"*

As a contemporary poet-epidemiologist-midwife, I am attracted to the grandeur of the sea, the innocence of childhood, the beauty of birth and the power of testimony. Like epidemiology, I'm concerned with truth and experiences that are deepest and truest in life.

In my most recent book On the Brink of the Sea, I write about love in our time of constant war and rising hate. It crosses over neat American borders into 21st-century wars and epidemics and plumbs a harsh (and humorous) childhood

Given my own childhood poverty as well as my work with MSF and Catholic Relief Services, all author royalties are donated to these two stellar humanitarian aid organizations.

A number of the poems were written while I was living in Cork, Ireland and travelling the countryside for work.

Your expertise is in epidemiology, can I ask what your thoughts are on how the pandemic has been handled in America currently?

If you'll forgive me, I hope to turn the question upside down. I would like to speak about America and Europe's actions regarding the Covid pandemic in Africa. How have we as affluent countries dealt with Covid in Africa?

So far Africa has been the continent least affected by Covid-19, however, now it's spreading beyond capital cities and lack of tests and other supplies are hampering responses.

> *"One of the most meaningful projects for me*
> *was WHO's development of survey tools*
> *to assess maternal and infant health*
> *in eight African countries"*

Importantly, epidemiologists warn of the catastrophic shortage of health care professionals and the drastic reduction of medical supplies because of border closures, price increases and restrictions on exports imposed during the pandemic.

The good news is aid organizations such as MSF Ireland are at the forefront of intervening in Africa and taking action.

Can you share any words of wisdom that helped you in your successful career?

A love of learning and desire for the common good inspired my career. My words of wisdom? Avoid pessimism as it lacks vision. Choose to hope as it sets one's heart on fire. And do not go into deep debt! Apply for internships, residencies, fellowships—think out of the box. Simply be the best that you can be.

JENNIFER CARROLL MACNEILL

Author, Barrister, Policy Advisor, TD

Contact:

Website:
www.jennifercarrollmacneill.ie
Twitter: CarrollJennifer

*D*id you always know from your secondary/third level school years that you would go down the path of politics or did something/someone decide that path for you?

I have always been very interested in current affairs which, I think, came from my mum who is keenly interested in politics, and was a big fan of Garret Fitzgerald.

I studied politics in college and went on to qualify as a solicitor. I then worked in government for several years and went on to complete further studies in political science. All that being said, I had never actually planned on becoming a politician myself.

The idea of putting myself forward for election hadn't occurred to me until I was asked by Fine Gael to run in the local election.

You have a range of occupations already including author, barrister, policy advisor and now TD, is there another vocation that you would like to add to your list of achievements?

I am privileged to have been elected as a TD, and I hope that I'll have this position for as long as the good people of Dun-Laoghaire afford me the opportunity to do so.

The pandemic came out of nowhere and people were shocked by its ability to stop the economy and the human race globally in its tracks. How has this affected your professional/personal life in general as it can also have the positive effect of being at home with your family?

As is the case for people across the country, and around the world, Covid 19 has had an impact on my professional and personal life. It has certainly been a strange time to begin a new role, bringing both challenges and opportunities.

As a public representative, meeting people face to face is a huge part of how I do my job. The opportunities to do this now are obviously extremely limited which means I've had to find ways to work around this. My reliance on video conferencing platforms for everything from team meetings to online clinics has hugely increased.

A positive that we can take away from our current situation is the fact that we have shown that working remotely, in many cases, is possible and sometimes more convenient. Personally, I have found that I am now able to attend meetings held during the evening as I can do so from my own home.

This is a huge benefit for me as the mother of a young child. I hope that the option of attending meetings and events online will remain once things begin to return to normal, offering us all a bit more flexibility and convenience.

Like everybody else that is working from home with young children, I am doing my best with what can be, at times, a challenging situation. While it's wonderful to have more time at home to spend with my son, juggling childcare duties while remaining productive and efficient can often be difficult.

In saying this, I am mindful of all those who are working on the frontlines and the vital work that they do in order for us to be able to stay at home and keep safe.

You are a passionate advocate for Women's Aid, this is an exposed time for people who are at home scared and a huge area of concern. You have also worked with Coercive Control Ireland to raise awareness. Will you consider other ways vulnerable people can be supported if this type of lockdown happens again in the future?

There is a range of vulnerable people that the current restrictions have had a particularly significant impact on.

I am thinking in particular of children with additional needs that have faced severe disruption to their routines, as well as children and adults that rely on ongoing care and therapy.

I have been appointed to the Special Dáil Committee on Covid-19 and will be raising all of these issues as I look to find practical solutions to help these individuals as early as can be done safely.

Can you share any words of wisdom that helped you in your successful career?

I think that the simplest advice is often the best. Find something that you're truly interested in and work extremely hard - it will take you a long way.

STEPHAN MURTAGH

Executive Coach, Exhibition Influencer

Contact:

Twitter: The Exhibition Guy

*W*e hear the term 'Influencer' many times on social media, you are known as the 'Exhibition Influencer'. Can you tell me what that means and what results business owners can benefit from this service?

Yes, we do seem to hear the term a lot these days, but I think the day of an "influencer" being purely a famous singer or model has changed thankfully. The role of an "influencer" today is more about sharing value about something you know well and are passionate about. I think it's way more than just selling products and services but rather how one can help shape an industry.

I see a lot more of the younger generation migrating to their friends as influencers and not just famous people. It's not a title I'm overly comfortable with as I'm just a real person who is incredibly passionate about what I do.

In business, the influencer word was replaced for a short time with "thought leader" – I have been described as a thought leader quite a bit. More recently I have been described as an "Exhibition Influencer" and think this comes from my deep understanding of what makes exhibitions and exhibitors get the best results from Trade Shows.

This is not borne from reading lots of books on the subject (although I do...2 books a week!) it comes from 30 years of walking thousands of aisles of Exhibition halls globally to understand how powerful our industry is and how my experience can make a real difference.

It's about shaping things that will make the next show even one percent better and how we are all learning each day. So, I think that if incredible passion and experience combined make you an influencer, I'm very happy to be called one.

> *"I have also always been interested in doing*
> *a TED Talk and this is one of my goals for the future"*

Can you give a summary of your career path to date as there are different areas like your sales training on LinkedIn that you share for free?

For almost 30 years I have been in the sales environment and it's a high-energy job, but I thrive on helping companies do better and it's the key reason we brought The Exhibition Guy to market. To combine the passion and experience so everyone wins.

In my sales career, I have sold Exhibitions, Yellow Pages, Radio, Print, Digital, and a brief stint in office equipment which I was dreadful at!! I'm more of a concept guy and selling physical products like office equipment just wasn't for me...in my sales career, I think I just realised that I preferred selling not what is but rather what will be if that makes sense.

I love working with clients on concepts and executing great delivery of training programs, looking at their problems, and coming up with solutions...of finding better ways of doing things.

"There's an old expression that says..." Nobody has ever become poor by giving" and I really buy onto this logic"

Aside from The Exhibition Guy business, I also have a company called Your Sales Coach Ltd which works with companies specifically in Sales, Marketing, Branding & social media.

Whilst my passion is for all things Exhibitions, running a small business for years has taught me all things sales & marketing, branding & social media.

When I set up The Exhibition Guy, I literally had no money for branding and marketing so had to go out and learn how to do it for free. When it comes to Marketing and Branding a small business, I am a big believer in sharing content on social media and looking for nothing in return because longer-term relationships are built upon becoming the expert and helping people.

I am a real person, not a salesperson and real people help each other...it`s that simple. Someone who is an expert in their field and my hope would be that when someone is doing an Exhibition that they would think of our business. This is why we do what we do and by sharing it with other people we are all winning.

How has the pandemic affected your business and how have you managed to keep busy?

The pandemic has obviously decimated the Exhibition industry and no question we are suffering badly however we are a very dynamic industry and if anything, it has shown us that we need to be better as an industry when we come out the other side.

We all need to have a better offer for our clients as they will demand and need more. As someone who trains mainly outside of Ireland and can't travel right now, it's had a strong effect on our business, but it's also given us a great opportunity to look at and make our offer even better.

I have never been busier, I have been training online for the past 18 months so luckily the whole online, zoom thing is not new to me. I was fortunate to be appointed a trainer for The Entrepreneurs Academy some time ago so am doing 2-3 courses a week for them currently along with some other clients abroad who are training their teams online.

Between a couple of training sessions, a week, developing new programmes, designing a website, social media content and working as a Team Leader on the Global Exhibition Think Tank for our industry, I can't see myself putting my feet up anytime soon.

Can you share any words of wisdom that you received that helped you in your successful career?

For me, my definition of success has changed quite a bit. It used to be all about money and having lots of clients and being perceived as successful. This just doesn't matter to me that much anymore and one of the biggest pieces of advice I could give to any business is not to chase the money...chase the passion and the money will follow.

Ironically, since I started to change my mind set to this, business has in fact been far better and I have been far happier.

I am just one person on a mission to help people in business and life and I am loving what I do, this helps me also be a better person. I think one thing I have learned about myself during Covid -19 and one piece of advice I would say is...Just be yourself...Everyone else is taken!

One hashtag that I have started using recently has really become my current day mantra and that is:

#LookToWhatYouCanDoNotWhatYouCant.

LUCY WOLFE

Sleep Consultant, Co-Creational Parent and Relationship
mentor

Contact:

Website: www.sleepmatters.ie
Instagram: Lucy Wolfe Sleep

*Y*ou are well recognised in your field of expertise, how and why did you choose this specific career path?

I came to this career following my own struggles with sleep deprivation with my oldest son who is now nearly 18.

As a new parent, I was disappointed to discover the lack of support in this area but also in the suggested approach of just leaving your baby to cry. This did not sit well with me and as I went on to have more children, I became more aware of the need to change the narrative and provide the level of support that I felt I needed then and so I pursued training, education and experience in order for that to happen.

I am in practice for 10 years now and have authored two books and I feel very privileged to accompany parents on their journey, nurturing their child's sleep to its best potential in a child-centered and holistic way.

You have stated you are not a fan of tough love, controlled crying and cry-it-out techniques to solve sleep problems in children. These are the longstanding techniques, what are the more current ones?

My own approach is to look at the whole story, acknowledging that there are so many influencing factors. By just addressing one aspect with a cry-intensive technique does not necessarily address the actual issues at play and may also cause unnecessary stress for the family unit.

By taking sleep into relevant segments, by helping parents gain a deeper understanding, by managing expectations that are individually orientated and age-appropriate and by honoring the internal body clock; transitions that can be made when necessary, with my stay and support approach.

This replaces the cry-it-out strategies and provides the child with loving comfort, support and co-created confidence. This together will result in the opportunity to gain a higher sleep ability with the partnership of the parent until they feel more safe and secure in the overall context of their sleep.

Have you found during the pandemic, a rise in messages looking for help at home especially now and perhaps in the foreseeable future, as families are mainly at home and working from home?

It has certainly been a good opportunity for many families to be able to make changes that sometimes seem unmanageable when we have day-care, commutes and work pressures.

Although those work pressures have remained and for some become even more challenging. For many, provided everyone has been healthy, they have certainly viewed it as a valued opportunity to grow their child' sleep tendency.

In your opinion and from your experience, is there any quick tip that new parents should know from the beginning to implement?

I encourage new parents to understand every child is different and unique and that building a loving trust bond/relationship is key.

Follow your instincts and listen to your own internal wisdom, respond to their signals and read the language of sleep so that you can ideally avoid overtiredness.

This may be indicated by brief eye rubs, yawns rather than intense symptoms. Remember that there is no right or wrong way, just what feels appropriate for you and your family unit and there is always opportunity within this.

Can you share any words of wisdom that helped you in your successful career?

I have found to aim high and compete only with yourself, placing a value on your time and expertise.

All the while maintaining an authentic, kind, compassionate and always curious mindset has helped my growth as both a person and a professional.

SIMON ACTON

Founder & Managing Director at Next Eco Car

Contact:

Website: www.nextecocar.ie

$\mathcal{C}$an you give a summary about what your business involves and where your passion for cars came from?

My business is about helping people transition to more sustainable transport options. Primarily, that is by selling electric and hybrid cars, but I don't see myself as a car salesman in the traditional sense. I see my role as educating people about the benefits of driving electric, both financially and environmentally and then helping them choose a vehicle which best suits their needs.

I then support them through the journey of their transition, typically that involves advising on charging options while also arranging finance if needed, extended warranties and other relevant matters. We provide a personalised end-to-end service.

My passion for cars undoubtedly came from my dad. He had raced in his earlier years and always had some car in the garage he was restoring while I was growing up. So, I inevitably developed an interest in anything with wheels and an engine.

I started racing karts at 11 years old in my school and continued into my 30's eventually competing in cars in a European endurance racing series. I stopped for financial reasons but would love to race again one day. Now I would understandably be looking at one of the electric racing series which are now starting to emerge.

> *"I also found myself working crazy hours*
> *and suffering badly with stress and insomnia*
> *which over a period of time led to depression"*

Your previous 'life' was quite a different profession, how did working in the IT industry lead you down the career you are in currently?

I worked in IT for 23 years altogether. I began as a software developer after graduating from university in 1994 and over time I worked in various different roles, eventually moving into project management. This is a route many career IT folk will be familiar with, but I eventually reached a point where I just wasn't enjoying what I was doing anymore. I missed the creative aspects of software development and was often frustrated in the management role by politics and bureaucracy.

I also found myself working crazy hours and suffering badly with stress and insomnia which over a period of time led to depression. I didn't understand what was happening at the time and it took a breakdown in 2016 and an abortive return to IT a year later for me to finally accept that I needed to do something different.

It took a while to figure out, but I knew I wanted to do something with cars as I was ultimately fascinated by technology and the natural world. One day all the pieces just fell into place in my mind, and I came up with the idea for Next Eco Car.

You have spoken very openly about your mental health in the past, was that time in your life a reason for diverting your career?

100%. If I hadn't changed my career, I'm honestly not convinced I'd be here now. I had become very unhappy in my previous career to the point it was making me ill. I tried to push myself through but in the end, I just couldn't do it anymore and I just felt like a total failure.

Determination and application had always got me through tough times in my career in the past but that just wasn't working any more.

At the time I felt totally trapped; I didn't know anything else.

I had spent my whole career in IT, and I had a big responsibility with a wife and two young children.

What I learned through extensive therapy was that I needed to do something which had meaning to me and that I was passionate about. I consider myself lucky that I was able to figure out what that was.

How has the pandemic affected your business, and do you feel the motor industry will recover in time?

Basically, from mid-March we had no sales for three months at what would normally have been our busiest time of year. Business is slowly coming back now but I've not managed to pay myself in 3 months, so it's been tough. We are lucky not to have too many overheads and we will bounce back. We believe that we are in the best possible motor industry niche moving forward.

The pandemic has led a lot of people to think more about the pollution they are causing by driving a petrol or diesel car.

With the lock down, cleaner air was evident globally and a lot of people are now rightly thinking about what they can do. Trends are already emerging to suggest that whilst car sales are still depressed generally, sales of electric and hybrid cars are increasing which is great news for us and the planet.

"One day all the pieces just fell into place
in my mind, and I came up with the idea
for Next Eco Car"

Can you share any words of wisdom that helped you in your successful career?

Three things: Listen. Be authentic. Say thank you.

These are such simple things to do and they cost nothing. So many people in business forget the obvious things. Most businesses are about people. You need to hear what your customers want and what your colleagues need to be successful.

Being authentic is so important, so many people wear a mask, I know I did for many years. But it's ok to need help or to make mistakes, so long as you learn from those experiences. People relate to people who can accept they have flaws because everybody does. Experience tells me that overconfident people are generally hiding something.

Thanking people is just polite, I've always thanked people.

It doesn't matter if they are just doing their job or what position they hold, be humble, grateful and smile!

AOIFE RYAN

Parent and Relationship Mentor at Insight Matters

Contact:

Website: www.aoiferyan.ie

"My work is an absolute privilege and I continue to be awed daily by my clients and the amazing nature of the Human Spirit."

ell us about your privileged vocation.

Being invited into an individual's interior world, in a mentoring session, is an absolute honor. Holding space for another is sacred. To bear witness to their pain, suffering, joy, …. All their emotions and experiences and to accompany them on their journey through it all is not only a joy it is privilege.

I am awed daily by the resilience, creativity, and wisdom of the human spirit. Everyone that comes through my door has lived a life and experienced so many different events.

They are all unique individuals.

When they come to me it is usually because things have become overwhelming or are just not working for them anymore. They have all found such incredible ways of coping with life, often times with extreme trauma. It is an honor to share that with them and to help them make sense of it all, so that they can move forward and find ways of being in the world that works better for them.

I believe strongly that we all know what we need to do for ourselves, and I work with people to help them build their trust in their inner knowing.

*"I often use the metaphors of 'putting
on your own oxygen mask first' or 'keeping
your emotional cup full'*

When working with children and parents, the focus commonly is the child/ren. You focus on the parent, sometimes there is not enough emphasis on the parent. What is your view on this?

For me, all parenting starts with self. You can only give to another (in this case your child/ren) what you have got for yourself. To help our children manage and regulate their emotions, they need a calm adult to regulate with and work through difficult emotions. When we parent ourselves and take care of our own needs we are teaching our children that they too need to care for themselves. When we acknowledge and express emotions it gives our children permission to acknowledge and express their emotions.

I believe that parents self-care is of paramount importance to their child's emotional/mental wellbeing. As parents, it is important to reflect on our own stories and understand why we behave in a particular way. We can then begin to understand why we may "react" to our children in particular ways, rather than responding.

When parents champion and take care of themselves, their relationships with their children will automatically improve. I often use the metaphors of 'putting on your own oxygen mask first' or 'keeping your emotional cup full'.

When you have your mask on and your cup is full you are going to be able to relate to everyone in your life in a more positive and conscious way.

Do you think, as a mother to two children, that your own experience adds that realism to your mentoring? How do you teach parents to love and care for themselves first?

I have lived a life and had many experiences. I have taken a lot of time and I continue to take time, to reflect on my experiences in life and with my family and with my own mentor.

I feel that this process of continuous personal reflection is of the utmost importance, personally but also professionally. It enables me to be more conscious and present with my clients. I have done the work they are doing. I have gone to the painful and difficult places I am asking them to go to. I have sat and examined my life and I have learned deeply from that examination.

So yes, I do think that my life experience, including my experience as a Mum, has given me insight and realism and adds to my mentoring. I am by no means a perfect parent and I am learning all the time. Some days I don't get anything right at all! I feel that being honest and truthful around that is important. I am doing my best, and I will keep trying to do better, but today, it is enough. That is a message that I want all parents to hear ... you are enough!

How did you find the pandemic affected you and your family, both on a personal level and a professional one?

My children loved the lockdown! They enjoyed being off school and all of us spending time together as a family. The weather was lovely, so we spent many days in the garden, nurturing our tadpoles and playing with our dog. We played games, we baked, we crafted, and we talked and danced and sang a lot. As time has progressed, we have found a gentle daily rhythm and it has been lovely.

I took the pressure off with school from the word go ... they did what they could do and wanted too, but with no pressure. Some days/weeks we did nothing at all!

As a family, we have really focused on connecting with each other and communicating about how we are feeling and what we need. I want the children to remember that although there was worry and heightened anxiety around, they felt safe. The "feeling" in the house is so important and I wanted our environment to be as stress-free as possible.

They have missed their grandad, my dad, and I have too! My husband has been working from home full- time and I have been working online with clients too. This has been difficult at times as we are sharing the office, and scheduling times etc. can be tricky.

I miss working face to face with clients, but the new online experience has been interesting and in the most part has worked well.

I found that lockdown gave me time to work on different things and develop business ideas that perhaps I would not have without lock down! There is an opportunity in everything! I am doing an MSc. so, I was busy working away on assignments and study for that.

A colleague and I ran a free parental support service to help struggling parents during the lockdown and that was extremely rewarding.

There are many parents that have been finding things exceedingly difficult so being able to 'give back' and offer them a space to express themselves and find support has been wonderful. I have enjoyed the "space" that lockdown created in all our lives.

I have missed friends and family but overall, I feel we have been lucky and it has been good for us as a family.

"I found that lockdown gave me time to work on different things and develop business ideas that perhaps I would not have without lock down. There is opportunity in everything"

Can you share any words of wisdom that helped you in your successful career?

"Trust your instinct" and "Whatever you are feeling is important and valid"

I feel that both these words of wisdom go hand in hand. So often we feel something, but we discount it and talk ourselves off in another direction.

But I have learned that my "gut instinct" or as I now call it, "my heart voice" is never wrong. What I am feeling is always right for me and I need to honor that and work with it.

That change to trusting myself, my inner feelings and not being swayed by the "outside" voices has been a huge learning point for me. It has been a positive point because now I am in the driving seat for me always.

Finding my voice in life took a long time, now that I have it, I want to use it to help myself and also to help and inspire others.

MURIEL BOLGER

Journalist and Award-Winning Travel Writer.

Contact:

Facebook: Muriel Bolger

*Y*ou have spoken about meeting many memorable characters, who was the most memorable character you met and why?

I've been incredibly lucky in my career, in that it satisfies many facets of my personality, I love socialising. I love people, I love travel and I love to read, and journalism for me has fed into all of those needs, in bucketfuls.

As a result, I've encountered weird, wonderful and totally whacky people. It's inevitable that some facets or ingredients of the people I've met or interviewed will make their way into the characters in my novels somewhere along the line.

I can't name a favourite person, but I do know I enjoyed meeting Jeffrey Archer, Robert Ludlum, Terry Wogan, Joanna Lumley and Peter Ustinov.

Could you write the title of your memoir/biography in three words, and would you share a short summary of its content if you have started one?

No, I haven't started a memoir yet. I'm too busy gathering things to put in one, should it ever materialise. What would I call it? In three words? Muriel – She Lived.

I suppose it would cover the eclectic parallel paths my life has taken as a happily married woman to being suddenly catapulted into single mum-hood with three petulant teenagers, to my five-star travel writing lifestyle.

Maybe Trains, Boats and Planes might be a better title.

Did you find it difficult to get your writing noticed or did male and female journalists have equal status while pursuing your Journalism career?

I didn't choose journalism or writing as a career. I came into it at 40, following my sudden marriage breakup. I had been a stay-at-home mother until then, which was the norm at the time.

I needed to work, and a friend told me about an ANCO (now FAS) course, called Women into Writing. I was accepted on this and got work experience in the features department with the Irish Press Group. I remember being very surprised at the way women and men had equal status in the newsroom.

It wasn't the case in most workplaces then. I suppose my career path was shaped during that time. I was sent on Ryanair's inaugural flight to

Paris, before it became a budget airline, and all the editors of every magazine and newspaper in Ireland were on it and suddenly I had contacts.

In that overworked cliché - the rest is history. Writing books and novels came much later.

What do you think of the term 'citizen journalist' and has social media been good for new, emerging writers/journalists?

I am skeptical about citizen journalism. I'm not convinced that it doesn't feed into that other term that I detest, 'fake news.'

Social media has changed things dramatically in the past decades and I've seen it greatly devalue the work of those who are serious about making a living from writing.

It has broadened the competition ridiculously and not always with quality material or factual matter either.

Now, more than ever, we need to be able to rely on the source of our news, and that's not the case.

"I did invite Prince Charles to tea at my gaffe, after meeting him in Powys Castle. He hasn't yet taken me up on my offer"

Can you share any words of wisdom that helped you in your successful career?

Starting out I was told, 'If you want to get on, get a name for being reliable, for being open to learning new things, and for never missing a deadline.'

And I couldn't agree more.

AOIFE MOLLIN

People and Personal Development Coach

Contact:

Website: www.amaresults.com

"Is this you? You are getting up for workday after day and you are wondering, "Why am I doing this? Is now the time to take a step back?"

his quote is from your website. How do you guide people on a different career path?

A lot of times people are in the habit of following the traditional path -School - College / University - Get a job - Get promoted - Get a mortgage - Feeling like I can't change my job because I have responsibilities.

When you are somebody who has followed that path without consciously making choices and understanding how you really want to live your life – you can end up stuck in a rut of just going into work and doing a job.

Sometimes a really good job, however, it stresses you out because you're not enjoying the work at all, and you know you want to do something different.

Usually, people then jump straight to looking for a new job and they move to a different company. After the novelty wears off after a few months, they're back to feeling stuck again.

When I work with people on their next career move, they get a chance to take a step back and really understand more about themselves. About what's important to them and how they want to live their lives. I help them to look at a different way of making decisions so that their life isn't always being impacted by their work.

They become really clear on what's important to them and how to make those decisions.

What was the turning point for you in your career bridging corporate finance and management consulting, advancing to coaching in people development?

Within my own career, there was a little bit of trial and error. I worked with great people when I worked in corporate. I was in London at the time and knew I wanted to move back to Ireland, so I just quit and moved home with no real plan.

A friend suggested management consultancy and when she told me about her job, I thought I have some of those skills, perhaps I can do that (It was also 2008 so I was lucky to get the job offer just before Lehman Brothers collapsed and we plunged into recession)

Within Management Consulting, a lot of my projects involved bringing changes into organisations and I saw how the middle managers struggled juggling all the different expectations. When I was managing a team there was so much, I needed to learn about leading a team that you're not really taught anywhere.

That is where my interest in working with middle and senior managers comes from – they are the squeezed middle who are managing expectations from the Directors / C-suites in the company and also managing expectations of their team.

I worked on several projects around training and leadership training which was how I realised I wanted to specialise in leadership development. Career coaching developed as I was coaching people in relation to leadership development.

*"Once people are clear and confident in their career strategy, it's then easier to start focusing
on developing themselves as a leader"*

What did you do next when you realised you needed a completely new career choice?

Some of the skills that I used in corporate finance (project management, dealing with clients, writing presentations, and reports) were the same skills needed in management consulting so while the careers are different, the skills are transferable.

That's how I work with my clients when career coaching – if my clients know the skills, they have that could potentially be transferable then it can be easier to make career decisions.

I had a plan when I started AMA Results in 2015 -the economy was really starting to pick up and I thought if I can't be successful with a company when the economy is good then I would have no chance at being successful owning my own company. I gave myself a year to go for it and five years later, it continues to do well.

How did the pandemic affect your business ethos, and did you have to be innovative in your future planning?

At the start of lockdown in Ireland, I had to move very quickly to show clients how I could still work online. Luckily about 25-30 per cent of my business was already online for the past three years so I already had systems set up in the background which made the transition easier.

The other 70 per cent of my business that was not already online was affected and I've continuously worked to move the rest of my business online during lockdown. Even though the restrictions are easing, the majority of businesses that I work with are still working from home.

I have updated some of my back-office systems and am currently working on updating my website to reflect online offerings.

Can you share any words of wisdom that helped you in your successful career?

Know what you want in life and then drive your own career. I had some great managers when I was working in London at the beginning of my career and one in particular always asked me what I wanted to learn and where I wanted to go in my career, I just wanted him to tell me what he thought I should do!

I really had no idea what I wanted. Before I left London, I did a job interview where I got asked the question "Where do you want to be in 5 years' time" and I gave a standard answer of progressing in the role and managing more people.

The guy who was interviewing me put down his sheet of paper and said "What is it that you really want to do…. I don't

think you know what you want…what hobbies do you want to have outside of work…where do you want to live…what do you want to give back to the community"

At the time I remember thinking he was weird…it took me a while to realise the importance of setting up the life you want for yourself. Your career is one part of that. When you do have an idea of what you want it is so much easier to navigate your own career.

I would like to thank all my guests in this book for sharing the highs and lows of their lives and businesses. If you have a story you would like to share about your business or about how you began your company – send me a message and let's continue the TLC journey. A special thank you to Wendy Stunt and Alan Hennessy for supporting my TLC idea in the early stages.

Connect with me here:
Website: www.yvonnereddin.com
Email: yvonne@yvonnereddin.com

Printed in Poland
by Amazon Fulfillment
Poland Sp. z o.o., Wrocław

12681816R00118